D0915108

THE LEARNING ADVANTAGE

THE LEARNING ADVANTAGE

Six Practices of Learning-Directed Leadership

Anna Kayes
Associate Professor, School of Business and Leadership, Stevenson University, USA

and

D. Christopher Kayes
Associate Professor, School of Business, George Washington University, USA

palgrave
macmillan

© Anna Kayes & D. Christopher Kayes 2011

All rights reserved. No reproduction, copy or transmission of this publication may be made without written permission.

No portion of this publication may be reproduced, copied or transmitted save with written permission or in accordance with the provisions of the Copyright, Designs and Patents Act 1988, or under the terms of any licence permitting limited copying issued by the Copyright Licensing Agency, Saffron House, 6–10 Kirby Street, London EC1N 8TS.

Any person who does any unauthorized act in relation to this publication may be liable to criminal prosecution and civil claims for damages.

The authors have asserted their rights to be identified as the authors of this work in accordance with the Copyright, Designs and Patents Act 1988.

First published 2011 by
PALGRAVE MACMILLAN

Palgrave Macmillan in the UK is an imprint of Macmillan Publishers Limited, registered in England, company number 785998, of Houndmills, Basingstoke, Hampshire RG21 6XS.

Palgrave Macmillan in the US is a division of St Martin's Press LLC, 175 Fifth Avenue, New York, NY 10010.

Palgrave Macmillan is the global academic imprint of the above companies and has companies and representatives throughout the world.

Palgrave® and Macmillan® are registered trademarks in the United States, the United Kingdom, Europe and other countries.

ISBN 978-0-230-57754-1

This book is printed on paper suitable for recycling and made from fully managed and sustained forest sources. Logging, pulping and manufacturing processes are expected to conform to the environmental regulations of the country of origin.

A catalogue record for this book is available from the British Library.

A catalog record for this book is available from the Library of Congress.

10   9   8   7   6   5   4   3   2   1
20 19 18 17 16 15 14 13 12 11

Dedication

For Brad and Ben

Contents

Preface

With just an hour before landing, the team had little time to reflect on their past success. Just short of reaching their destination, they began to experience problems that threatened the current success of their mission. First, they lost direct communication with key members of their team. Then, the computer, which monitored descent and tracked their progress, appeared to be malfunctioning. The engineers at headquarters could no longer rely on the computer for accurate updates on the location of the remotely located team. No one had seen a project like this before. They faced a task both novel and complex. To arrive at this place and time involved 400,000 individuals working around the clock for nearly five years. The average age of the team members was only 26 years and few of them had significant leadership experience, but they had learned from their experience, and this would have to be enough.

The engineering team collaborated and identified the source of the computer problem. The mission had overworked the computer, but the calculations were fine. Eventually the team regained contact with their peers at their remote location. With less than a minute to landing, another problem arose. The remote team peered out of the window and noted rocks strewn over the intended landing point. They called off the landing and boldly searched for another site—but yet another problem emerged. Only a minute of usable fuel remained. If the team couldn't land within seconds, the entire mission would be aborted. In practice runs, the engineers at mission control led the landing. But the situation had changed. The engineers handed off the landing to the crew inside the lunar module in an act of extreme trust. With just 14 seconds of fuel left, the two-man crew lowered the Eagle lunar module a mere 252,088 miles from its original point of liftoff.

The team didn't celebrate just yet; they still needed to return to earth. But they did exchange short controlled looks of measured confidence. Even though they had landed the first person on the moon, the team remained determined not to lose focus until everyone returned safely back to earth (Discovery Channel, 2008; Kranz, 2000).

The teamwork, learning, and leadership that accomplished the first lunar landing illustrate the advantage of learning. Relying on past experience is never enough. In the face of novel and complex problems, learning becomes an essential part of the leader's toolkit.

While few leaders will undertake projects as complex and novel as a mission to the moon, all leaders share something in common. Just as the successful moon landing required learning, so do more-common leadership situations. The practices displayed by the NASA Apollo moon mission included trust by leaders and followers, trial and error learning, resilience in the face of setbacks, team learning in the face of complexity, learning from limited experience, and the ability to manage emotions productively. Whether directing a sales force into new markets, cleaning up in the wake of a disaster, or navigating the politics of a consulting project, leadership requires learning. This book describes how leaders, working in a variety of contexts, rely on learning to solve complex problems.

Acknowledgments

We would like to recognize and thank our many colleagues and friends who are committed to the value of learning and to all those leaders who were willing to share their stories of their struggles and successes with learning in their organizations. Some of those who have contributed to our thinking and supported our writing include the following: Dr. David Kolb and Dr. Richard Boyatzis who have acted as our mentors, collaborators, and friends for over a decade. It is from their work—moving these ideas forward—that we draw inspiration. Dr. Russ Vince and Dr. Michael Reynolds have recognized the potential contribution of these ideas from the start as well and have been generous with their time and feedback to revise our thinking. Dr. James Bailey, Dr. Deborah Leather, and Dr. Paul Lack provided encouragement and logistical and institutional support for this project. Dr. Natalie Houghtby-Haddon and Jim Robinson at the Center for Excellence in Public Leadership have been at the forefront of integrating learning approaches to developing leaders. They have influenced thousands of leaders around the importance of learning. In particular, thank you to Lauren Gordon for her graphic artistry, Cindy Orticio for her detailed eye and feedback on the manuscript, and our family who supported us with patience while we wrote. Also, a thank you to Stephen Rutt for seeing the potential in our ideas on leadership.

Introduction

Leadership and riding a bike

To illustrate the difficult task of learning to be a leader, we want to begin by sharing a personal story on learning and leadership. The story helps clarify our own philosophy about learning and the role of the leader. One weekend, several years ago, we tried to "teach" our oldest son to ride a bike. Since we are both educators and have done quite a lot of research on how people learn, we thought we could apply some of what we know to this situation. After two days on the school parking lot, we got a lesson in leadership and learning.

We began by thinking like learners. So we defined our purpose, our "learning goal" in popular parlance. Our learning goal was simple: to see our son ride his bike without our help and without the use of training wheels. We thought about our method as well. We would hold the back of his seat, or perhaps grab his handlebars and help him find his balance, and run alongside the moving bike. Finally, we knew that creating the right environment for learning was important. So we entered this process with patience and determination, knowing that he would have many stumbles and falls and that we would not let small setbacks get in the way of achieving our objective.

We began by watching him mount his bicycle, newly freed from the constraints of its training wheels. He had difficulty even sitting on the bike at a standstill with his toes touching the ground. The whole thing seemed foreign and uncomfortable to him. But we insisted that he persist and explained to him that we would push him while he tried to balance the bike. We assured him that we would be right behind him, holding on to his seat to catch him if he went off balance.

After about 20 minutes of running next to him, both of us (who are in fairly good condition) had maxed out our heart rates and were past the threshold level for our age. So we had to stop. Even taking turns, we quickly realized that it is impossible for a person to run bent parallel to the ground alongside a bike for more than a few minutes in the summer heat without reaching dangerous pulmonary conditions. Tired and frustrated, we moved to rest on the curb while our son pulled his bike next to us. So we moved to relax in the shade and we each enjoyed a nice cool fruit drink from a box.

After our rest, we encouraged him to get back on the bike and try a few more laps around the parking lot. By now, the bees had discovered the fruit drinks. They must have smelled it on our hands because they followed us out into the parking lot—a huge distraction for our son, who is fascinated by but also deathly afraid of bees. Our calming words "to ignore the bugs" and focus on riding did not seem to reassure him much. He took a second break as we shooed the bugs away. Now that we both had regained a survivable standing heart rate, we took turns holding onto the bike while our son peddled through the parking lot. He began to show a little success. He glided for a few seconds, unassisted. We encouraged a couple of more laps around the parking lot, but he didn't seem interested in continuing. As we walked back to the car, we, learners always, began to question this experience. What in our method did not work? Did we set a goal that was too ambitious? Did we not have the right lesson plan? Did our own anxiety create an environment where he could not learn? Should we have been more encouraging? Perhaps, we concluded, we didn't understand what he wanted to accomplish.

On the next day, we loaded the bicycle back into the SUV, headed to the school parking lot, and started again. About 30 seconds into the first push, something kicked in and within about 20 feet of us propping him up, our son began to float. He wobbled—often appearing like a duckling moving into the water for the first time, wiggling back and forth—but underneath the tremor, the bike began to swim. He swam over the patchwork of shade spread across the asphalt. His loud cheers of excitement must have been heard through the surrounding neighborhood. He learned to ride just in time; we were tired from his efforts but still had enough energy to jump up and scream in joy.

In our joy, we wanted to give our son a big hug for his effort and perseverance. We screamed, "Come back here, come back here! Come give us a hug. We are so proud!" But 8-year-olds will quickly trade a hug for the excitement of their first bike ride. We ran after him in victory, and he smiled back in happy defiance under the glowing green helmet. He rode away not just because that was the only way he could ride, but also because he wanted to get away. He wanted to ride the bike by himself. He didn't want us holding him up—or, more importantly, holding him back. He wanted to ride on his own. He had achieved his goal; he found pleasure in his new ability to balance his bike. It was fun and it was his.

We, on the other hand, retreated to the shady corner of the parking lot and watched in both joy at what we had seen and in horror of what might happen. Maybe we should buy knee and elbow pads, we thought, as we watched him take his first scary spill that landed him a scratched-up knee. What if he accidentally rides into the street? It was too late for such thoughts. He now rode on his own.

This was quite a lesson for us. It challenged much of what we thought we knew about learning and taught us something about leadership. Ultimately, we learned that we could not teach our son to ride his bike. At the core, only he could motivate himself. It didn't matter how badly we wanted him to ride, the choice to learn was his. We may have helped him keep his balance as he learned to manage the bike, but no instructions really helped much. It was something he had to learn for himself. We couldn't explain to him how to ride the bike, even though each of us has ridden for years. Our encouragement was helpful; at times we were tempted to point out his slow progress, and to compare him to his peers, but we kept these criticisms to ourselves. We had created an environment where he could learn, where he was not criticized for doing things at his own pace, and where learning, although risky, was full of rewards. We were there to celebrate his learning, and that was enough.

When he finally learned how to balance unassisted, he never looked back. He kept going forward and quickly forgot about the help we gave him. He rode away so that we could no longer keep up with him. It didn't matter; we wouldn't have been able to keep up with him in the long run. Even the bees, which seemed to dampen his spirit the day prior, failed to have any lasting impact.

We hope that in reading this book you will find the same joy in the learning process as a leader that you had when first mastering something unfamiliar, like riding a bike, and that you will remember to celebrate the learning successes of others, whatever their pace.

Challenging your thinking about leadership

Reading this book may challenge your thinking about leadership. Throughout the book, we present studies, tell stories of leaders, and reference theoretical insights to rethink the role of learning in leadership. The book presents the following certainty. In today's complex world, learning is not simply a luxury, but a central task of leadership. For example, a study of partners in a major professional services firm (Boyatzis, 2006) confirmed that valuing and facilitating learning were the leadership skills that correlated most highly with performance. For those who lead in the face of complex and novel situations, learning proves one of the most important leadership practices.

By reading this book, leaders will see how to enlist learning as part of their everyday leadership practice. Learning is no longer a secondary activity, something to be attended to when all else is managed. Leaders need learning to survive and thrive. Current leaders as well as emerging leaders in a variety of situations can turn to this book to improve their understanding of leadership and to build leadership capacity. This book will be useful to leaders who

- ▶ Value learning by fostering learning in self and in others
- ▶ Engage in learning on an ongoing basis
- ▶ Seek to build learning as an ongoing part of organizational processes
- ▶ Strive to improve and grow each day
- ▶ Fight to improve performance.

In addition to placing learning at the center of leadership practice, this book challenges other widely held wisdom on leadership. For example, the "law of 10,000 hours" (see Ericsson and Lehmann, 1996) states that to master a task and achieve expertise requires 10,000 hours of deliberate practice. This law may hold true for developing expertise in specific, well-structured tasks such as chess, soccer, or even medical diagnosis, where experts must learn to master well-defined tasks. In situations of leader development, however, the "expert" rule rarely holds true. Leaders, in contrast to other types of "experts," need to develop higher-order learning processes and deal with competing commitments, the types of problems that other experts shun. Typical experts narrow their span of skills in order to gain expertise, whereas leaders need to widen and deepen their skill set in order to lead in the face of multiple, often competing, demands.

In addition to challenging conventional wisdom, the book offers concrete tools to improve leadership. In one case, we explore how attempts by personnel to improve medical safety not only rely on learning but also build learning into everyday tasks (Pronovost and Vohr, 2010). This book explains how leaders foster organizational learning and infuse learning into routine practices that pay-off for the organization as a whole.

Throughout this book, you will meet leaders who learn in the face of complex and novel situations:

- ▶ An army officer embeds himself into infantry teams in Iraq to study the importance of constant learning in combat.
- ▶ The managing partner of a major law firm trusts his new employee to start a new office in Japan and finds it thriving a decade later.
- ▶ A newly minted physician learns to navigate the challenges of a consulting firm.
- ▶ The head of a publishing empire navigates changes in the industry to innovate ahead of the competition.

Throughout the book we will relate stories of leaders. Some of these stories are based on interviews with leaders and we reference these stories as such. Other stories represent composite characters, or stories that reflect real situations but are not based upon real individuals. We reference these stories as based on composite characters. We use these stories and the technique of relying on composite characters to illustrate how leaders can overcome some of their limitations and improve their leadership.

Like these exemplary leaders, many of today's successful leaders rely on learning to gain the advantage in every walk of life. Whether improving their own leadership practices or improving the leadership capacity of others, leaders who engage learning thrive.

Learning-directed leadership: A new direction for leaders

The notion of learning-directed leadership challenges conventional wisdom because it both integrates traditional approaches to leadership and, at the same time, offers a fresh look at the work of leaders. Traditional leadership approaches often focus on only one dimension of leadership. Learning-directed leadership builds on all three fundamental dimensions of leadership: the leader, the led, and the context (see Figure 1). In addition, learning-directed leadership explains how leaders build learning capacity in each of these three areas. Improving individual learning capacity, building learning capacity in others, and engage their context as the basis for sustained learning. This is the work of the learning directed leader.

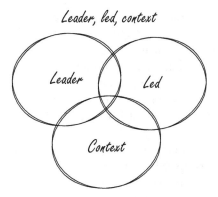

Figure I **Leader, led, context**

Failure to learn along these three dimensions can lead to disastrous consequences. This is what happened in May 1996. Eight climbers from four teams died as they pushed for the summit of Mount Everest, the world's tallest mountain. The events left climbers and observers alike searching for answers. Within the course of just a few hours, team members became separated. Leaders, exhausted from the push to the summit, began to make poor decisions, like not enforcing turnaround times. Assistant guides and team members faced a situation for which they were not prepared. Luckily for some, a few team members pulled together to coordinate one of the most daring rescue attempts on record to save the remaining stranded climbers.

The details of some of the shortfalls of traditional leadership practices appear in an analysis of this disaster in the book *Destructive Goal Pursuit: The Mount Everest Disaster* (Kayes, 2006). One explanation for the disaster is that the group members failed to adapt to the changing context. Their goal, described generally as to get to the top of the mountain, served as the source of identity for the team. Over the course of the six-week climb to the summit, however, the shared meaning on the team broke down. Individual team members believed they could get to the summit independently of one another. Leaders and team members alike failed to learn. From our study of teams like those on Everest, we begin to see the challenges of leadership in the face of complex and novel situations. Consider former US Treasury Secretary Henry Paulson during the financial meltdown of 2008. He had spent decades as an investment banker promoting free markets and limited government intervention. Capitalism and the power of market forces were a deeply held belief. Yet, acting as the chief regulator in the face of one of the worst financial crisis of his lifetime, his beliefs were put to the test. He chose government intervention into the banking system over the free market. The lesson: A leader must learn to adapt to the changing environment.

Learning-directed leaders engage the practices, beliefs, and ideas of learning. The reliance on learning stands in contrast to other approaches to leadership, like those that focus on influence, power, and often coercion. Learning-directed leadership emphasizes how leaders gather, process, and adapt to knowledge and involve others in this process. Learning-directed leadership values the practices of learning, not simply the outcomes of leadership.

Learning-directed leadership offers several advantages over traditional approaches to leadership. First, it focuses on the inherent potential in people to grow, to learn, to adapt, and to change for the better. The learning approach offers resources and knowledge designed to explain this process as well as its limitations. Learning-directed leadership advocates that leaders should be active participants in the process and not stand on the sidelines expecting learning to happen automatically. Some believe that learning leadership requires copying behaviors of leadership, but that people are pretty much fixed in their abilities. In contrast, our approach shows that with motivation to learn, any leader can lead through learning and generate new meaning from their experiences.

Also, the learning-directed approach to leadership is comprehensive. Many approaches to leadership—for example, the goal-setting approach offered by Gary Latham and Ed Locke (2006)—promise only a short-term solution to simple problems. The goal-setting approach is representative of the shortfalls of traditional leadership. Its principles remain too simplistic and too narrow to address most contemporary leadership problems. A standard of leading in the command and control world of the last century, goal-setting, and its many offshoots such as management by objective, have proven too myopic as stand-alone leadership tools. Goal setting, like so many other management practices, can be useful as one tool, but it is not a complete method for leadership.

By taking a learning-directed approach, leaders still rely on goals but they also learn to manage multiple competing goals, shift directions when necessary, and constantly evaluate progress. Leadership involves identifying the most important aspects of a task, those elements critical to success. In and of itself, traditional leadership processes sacrifice breadth of understanding in favor of focused attention (Ordóñez, Schweitzer, Galinsky, and Bazerman, 2009). Leaders that focus on specific, predefined goals are likely to lose touch with the bigger problem. From a learning perspective, this means that leaders must be able to exploit existing advantages while also exploring new opportunities (March and Simon, 1958). In short, a narrow and short-term focus encouraged by traditional leadership can lead to a myopic view of the leadership task. Effective leadership requires a dual focus. The leader must possess the fortitude to pursue a narrow and important task, but must simultaneously comprehend how a goal fits into a larger context. Learning-directed leadership offers a means to accomplish this dual-minded thinking.

Yet another advantage of the learning-directed approach lies in its acceptance of alternative sources of knowledge in the form of emotions, hidden assumptions, and conflicting goals. Traditional leadership practices assume that leadership is a rational process and that organizations function in rational ways. For example, goal-setting approaches propose that organizational goals can be broken down into smaller, individual goals, and individual goals can be generalized into organizational goals. The learning-directed approach to goal setting does not assume that the decision-making process in organizations is or should be rational. The data and knowledge needed for decisions are not always rational and quantitative, as organizations involve emotions, hidden assumptions, or self-contradictory goals (see Schein, 1978).

Six practices of learning-directed leadership

Many leaders seek a formulaic template to guide their actions. They often turn to accepted, well-established practices and overly simplistic formulas. While these practices can serve a leader well in some situations, leaders that engage in shifting and complex environments will find that many traditional leadership tools fall short. The results of such misdirected efforts often prove disastrous. What a leader needs is not a simple template, but a systematic way to assess, update, and change direction during the course of leadership.

Learning-directed leadership offers an alternative to overly simplistic guides for leadership behavior. We synthesize into six 'practices' the wide breadth and depth of leadership research that relates to learning. This book outlines these six learning practices of leaders:

▶ *Learning from experience.* Leaders recognize that experience is a starting point but not enough; today's leaders draw on experience to develop new insights, innovate, and change. Leaders help others recognize, reflect upon, and grow from their experiences.

▶ *Developing higher-order learning.* Leaders demonstrate a need for constant improvement through deliberate practice, constantly recognizing their own limits and continually managing competing commitments. At the same time, leaders help others improve their capacity to learn by working with them to recognize that most problems don't have clear answers and that they can't make everyone happy with each decision.

▶ *Building resilience.* Leaders learn to build adaptive practices, accept mistakes, thrive in the face of setbacks, and build on past failures. Leaders help others to overcome challenges, build confidence in their abilities, and succeed in the face of fear.

▶ *Fostering emotional intelligence.* Leaders understand the importance of emotions in themselves and others and learn to manage these emotions. Leaders improve the emotional intelligence of others by advocating for increased awareness and emotional management.

▶ *Fostering team learning.* Leaders rely on teams to get things done. Leading a team means learning and adapting. Leaders move beyond

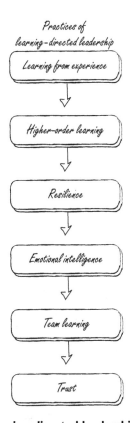

Figure 2 **Six practices of learning-directed leadership**

simple team-building to fostering skills and behaviors that encourage learning.

▶ *Nurturing trust.* Leaders know that trust, not coercion or force, is the currency of leadership. Leaders help others by creating an environment where unpopular views are heard and mistakes recognized regardless of the person's position in the organization.

These practices, outlined in Table 1 as well as Figure 2, offer leaders the opportunity to gather, process, update, and act upon new knowledge.

The learning-directed leadership cycle

Taken as a whole, these six practices constitute a starting point for leaders who wish to integrate learning into their leadership practice. One way to integrate these practices is to follow the learning-directed leadership cycle.

Table 1 **Six practices of learning-directed leadership**

Practice	Relationship to learning	The leader level	Practice with others
Learning from experience (*gathering and processing knowledge*)	Describes the four-fold process of learning from experience including direct experience, reflection, cognition, and experimentation.	Leaders understand their own unique preferences, skills, and abilities to learn.	Leaders engage in conversational learning to help others learn from their own unique experiences.
Developing higher-order learning (*processing knowledge in more complex ways*)	Describes how leaders develop higher-order thinking as they progress through continually more complex levels.	Leaders learn to view problems from a systems perspective, understand the value of ambiguity and paradox, and engage in complex decision-making.	Leaders develop followers to be innovative knowledge processors and engage in complex decision-making.
Building resilience (*meeting new challenges in learning, recovering from failure and setbacks*)	Describes the importance of adaptive practices, learning from failure, overcoming hardship, and responding to setbacks.	Leaders learn to focus on their own resilience during change, personal and professional setbacks, and crises.	Leaders learn to use a variety of tools to help their followers build resilience during change, setbacks, and crises.
Fostering emotional intelligence (*integrating the role of emotions in gathering and processing knowledge and meeting new challenges*)	Describes the role of emotions in learning, how to harness the power of emotions to learn more effectively, how to overcome deeply seated psychological barriers to learning, and how to use emotions to meet new challenges.	Leaders learn to develop awareness of their own emotions and how they help and hinder learning.	Leaders learn to enable followers to become more emotionally productive through self-reflection and greater self and social awareness.

Fostering team learning (*understanding the social nature of learning and overcoming social barriers to learning*)	Describes how leaders come to appreciate the social nature of learning and how to develop beliefs and skills that lead to effective social interaction.	Leaders learn to identify dysfunctional team processes and build beliefs and behaviors that lead to effective teamwork. Leaders develop the ability to master conversational learning to guide followers.	Leaders help followers build effective team structures using shared goals, roles, and decision making and working with their unique context and work to overcome barriers to team learning, such as groupthink, the Abilene paradox, and destructive goal setting.
Nurturing trust (*overcoming barriers to gathering and processing knowledge*)	Describes how leaders build the optimal environment for learning to occur. Barriers to trust (such as fear, blame, and conflict) are barriers to learning.	Leaders learn to create the optimal environment for learning, including building a "psychologically safe" culture.	Leaders engage others to create a safe culture to surface errors and mistakes, reflect, and learn.

The cycle integrates thinking from Kolb's (1984) learning cycle with the six practices and also contains additional considerations (see Kayes, 2002). The process describes a continuous cycle, as leaders should revisit each step. Like the learning cycle, the learning-directed leadership cycle presents a normative process. This means the cycle is an idealized version of leading and should not be considered an end in and of itself but part of a larger toolkit. The five-step cycle provides a general guide that integrates the various practices introduced in upcoming chapters (see Figure 2).

STEP 1: ASSESS SITUATION COMPLEXITY

Most leadership processes begin by defining desired outcomes or setting outcomes. The learning-directed approach suggests a different starting point: understanding the nature of the context or task before defining outcomes. In the first phase, the leader assesses the situational complexity. She asks the following questions: Is the situation a puzzle or a mystery? Is the situation an ill-structured or well-structured problem? Is the situation faced a novel or routine task? Each of these questions is described in Chapters 1 and 4. If the situation is novel, it is unlikely that traditional goal setting will be helpful because there are no or few known ingredients to success. On the other hand, if the situation is routine, then the situation might lend itself to accepted practices.

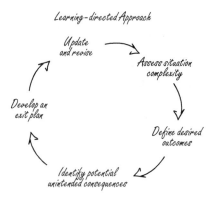

Figure 3 **The learning-directed leadership cycle**

STEP 2: DEFINE DESIRED OUTCOMES

Only after the situational complexity has been assessed does the leader begin to define desired outcomes. The desired outcomes must be considered in the context of the organization or environment; otherwise, they become too simplistic. Another important consideration is capability and resources. Will attempts to achieve the goal overstretch resources and capabilities? Only after an assessment of resources, environment, and capability can the leader rightly define the desired outcomes. Many leaders find the first two steps counterintuitive because they are often taught to define objectives first. Situational awareness should come after defining outcomes, they believe. Define desired outcomes only after assessing the situation may go against common practice. Only by assessing the situation first can the leaders then responsibly move forward with future defining tasks like setting goals and a vision. In actuality, we have observed how many leaders informally assess their situation before defining goals as a matter of course. The learning-directed leadership cycle makes this process explicit. Chapter 4 on higher-order learning provides more details on the process of making implicit assumptions explicit. Chapter 3 on learning from experience also describes the learning cycle and its usefulness as a leadership tool.

STEP 3: IDENTIFY POTENTIAL UNINTENDED CONSEQUENCES

The learning-directed leadership cycle considers the potential unintended consequences of pursuing the goal. The process involved in realizing unintended consequences provides a sharp contrast to the traditional goal-setting process. The magic that emerges from a goal-setting process can be seen in how it focuses the leader and the follower on narrowly defined, even simple aspects of tasks. By concentrating resources on these aspects of the task, leaders improve their chance of reaching the goal. The unfortunate consequence is that other aspects of the task are often ignored. Take the 1996 Mount Everest disaster. The teams focused so much effort on getting to the top of the mountain that they failed to devote the necessary resources to getting back down. The problem of climbers getting trapped or experiencing problems on the descent is so pervasive that climbers have developed a catch phrase: "Getting to the top is optional, getting down is not." This reminds them that the danger isn't just in reaching the summit, but in the unintended or unforeseen consequences of the goal. The problem of misdirected resources in climbing is so pervasive that the conventional wisdom, although hard to verify, is that 80 percent of climbing accidents happen on the descent (see Simpson, 2004, for an example).

Traditional leadership practices often fail to account for these nasty unintended consequences (see for example Latham and Locke, 2006). Unlike traditional goal setting, which fosters a narrow and limited view of a leader's role, the learning-directed approach focuses on understanding the task in its entirety. This provides a more complete picture. Leaders who engage the learning cycle force themselves to consider the unseemly side effects that emerge when pursuing goals. One question the leader may ask in this phase is: How will achieving the goal impact other areas or other competing goals? Chapter 4 thoughtfully considers the different types of learning and how they apply in different situations.

STEP 4: DEVELOP AN EXIT PLAN

An exit plan is similar to a stop rule common in engineering. An exit plan considers, ahead of time, what factors require a reevaluation of a current course of action. By building an exit plan for the early stages of the goal-setting process, a leader can overcome some of the psychological and social pressures associated with goal setting. One psychological factor that makes it difficult to abandon a goal is the tendency for leaders to escalate commitment (Staw, 1981). As leaders and their organizations become psychologically invested in a particular course of action, they tend to invest more resources into a project even as it seems to be a lost cause. Likewise, social pressures that arise from public expectations can also lead to fear of abandoning or changing a goal once a course has been established. A leader can turn to Chapter 8 on trust to find ways to build an environment that allows for changes in the course of action and creates a safe environment to test assumptions.

STEP 5: UPDATE AND REVISE

A hallmark of learning-directed leaders rests in their ability to update and revise past viewpoints. Leaders can find direction on this practice in Chapter 3 on learning from experience as well as Chapter 5 on resilience. In these chapters you will find examples of leaders who update and revise their thinking to achieve success. Throughout the learning-directed leadership cycle, leaders will rely on their ability to motivate and build direction. Leaders can turn to Chapter 6 on emotional intelligence as well as Chapter 7 on team learning to find more details about these practices.

Organization of the book

Chapter 1 introduces the importance of learning in organizations and among leaders. The chapter outlines several key reasons why learning has emerged as a key tool in the leadership toolkit. The complexity and novelty of today's leadership environment necessitate learning-directed, rather than traditional, leadership practices.

Chapter 2 focuses on the underlying conceptual basis of learning. The chapter presents four key approaches to learning and describes the relevance of each for learning-directed leadership.

Chapters 3 through 8 offer illustrations, examples, research, and underlying ideas behind the six practices of learning-directed leadership. We devote an entire chapter to each practice to help readers understand the basic principles and how they can be applied. Within each chapter are "Questions for reflection," which offer the reader a chance to reflect on the key points of each chapter, check for understanding, and think about the contents in the context of their own leadership practices. Sections within each chapter called "Strategies for leaders" provide exercises for introducing these chapter concepts into leadership practice or provide templates to further apply the ideas in the chapter. Each chapter begins with a leader's story that introduces readers to some of the leaders that inspired our book. This allows the reader to learn directly from these leaders' experiences. These chapters also include references to research studies that further support the practices. Whether learning to ride a bike, helping others build their leadership capacity, or kick starting one's own performance as a leader, learning-directed leadership provides a framework for improving leadership. If you are a leader interested in improving each and every day, learning from the latest research and theory, and revisiting some of the classic approaches to leadership in a contemporary way, the ideas in this book promise to be a permanent part of your leadership toolkit.

1 Learning in Organizations

Key ideas

▶ In a complex, information-rich, and dynamic organization, effective leadership requires continuous learning.

▶ Traditional approaches focus on power, influence, and motivation as the keys to leadership. These are important factors but prove less consequential in today's environment. Contemporary leaders rely on learning to navigate complexity and novelty. This is learning-directed leadership.

▶ Learning-directed leadership offers strategies to aid leaders as they learn from their experiences, constantly update their viewpoint, and challenge themselves and others to create new knowledge.

Leadership involves learning in a rapidly changing, complex, and challenging environment. This chapter draws on examples from the medical profession and the financial industry to illustrate the importance of learning-directed leadership. The examples show how today's leaders learn in organizations. The basis of leadership is shifting from positional power, formal authority, and influence to knowledge, expertise, and creativity. The chapter explains how leaders in many different types of organizations achieve the learning advantage in information rich, high-stakes, and changing environments.

A leader's story: Geeta's transitions from physician to consultant

Geeta, a recent medical school graduate and MBA student, took an unconventional path to leadership. After spending a good part of her adult life studying to be a physician, she decided that she wanted to make a bigger contribution to her field. Patient care had always been important to her, but she sought to make an impact on the broader profession as well. After some searching, and with the support of her family, she decided to take a position at a consulting firm promoting medical awareness and influencing health policy. Her first year, unsurprisingly, proved a challenge. Her medical training and few short years of practice served her well as she advised clients on the growing concern about "swine flu" and other medical issues. Navigating the competitive culture of a consulting firm proved another matter. In the world of medicine, success is often measured in ambiguous outcomes such as patient care and satisfaction. These ambiguous outcomes exist in the consulting world too, outcomes such as "client satisfaction," are difficult to achieve. As an additional challenge, she decided to maintain a part-time private medical practice while she built her consulting practice.

Over the course of the two years that we worked with Geeta, we watched her work through her role as both physician and consultant. Many people might have retreated from their ambition of educating the public about health care issues by returning to the comfort zone of private practice. Instead, Geeta adopted a learning-directed approach to achieve her goals. She quickly learned the formal rules as well as the important informal rituals of the consulting firm. She spent extra time consulting with her clients and observing senior partners in action. She consulted with friends, sought the help of trusted advisors, and faced each new experience as a learning opportunity. While all this was happening, she continued to stay up to date on the latest medical advances by reading medical journals as she returned from work each night on the commuter train.

We have worked with hundreds of leaders like Geeta, who rely on learning to navigate the challenges of leadership. In contrast to Geeta, we have unfortunately also seen too many individuals who have failed to learn. Many examples stand in contrast to Geeta. Consider managers who are promoted to a leadership position because of strong technical skills. Many of these managers mistakenly think that being an expert in the field automatically translates to effective leadership. The irony is that many leaders like this are recognized for their technical expertise and find themselves promoted to a position that requires a completely different set of skills. They find that the skills they have, those that helped them excel in their prior position, are of little relevance in the complex role of leader.

One of the key factors distinguishing leaders like Geeta from other leaders is that she successfully adapted to the new and changing demands of her role. Many leaders fail to learn from their mistakes, and as a result they never reach their full potential as well. Leaders that fail to reach their full potential prevent their employees from reaching their full potential. Without a good mentor or leader in their department, employees look elsewhere for leadership. Eventually, the organization itself suffers. This book is about helping individuals reach their full potential as leaders by focusing on how leaders learn and how they develop learning capacity in others. Taking the time to invest in learning is paramount, especially when leaders are weighed down with the day-to-day burdens of information overload, high-stakes decisions, and change.

The leadership context: "big data," high stakes, and change

The information-intensive, complex, and dynamic world presents unique challenges for leaders. Never before has information been so readily available but knowledge been so difficult to create. Some have called the information-intensive but knowledge-starved situation the world of "big data" and the consequence a resulting "data exhaustion" (*Economist*, 2010). The world of big data isn't the only element challenging leaders. Table 2 provides a quick list of the demands faced by today's leader, based on the work of James Reason (1995). Reason is an authority on learning in high-stakes fields and has identified characteristics that describe a complex leadership environment. Along the same lines, a study sponsored by the American Management Association (2007) reported that 82 percent of organizations surveyed thought the pace of change had increased in the previous 5 years and that at least one major disruptive change had occurred that had affected their organization in the last year (p. 3).

In the world of big data, high-stakes, and disruptive change, learning becomes essential for leadership. Once thought to be useful only in the domain of high-risk and high-stress occupations, learning is now a leadership requirement. Reason may have been concerned with high-risk leadership situations, but he could have easily been referring to any leader. In fact, contemporary leaders in business organizations share many of the challenges faced in well-known, high-stress, and high-consequence positions such as pilots, surgery teams, and military quick reaction forces (e.g., Hanna, Uhl-Bien, Avolio, and Cavarretta, 2009).

From solving puzzles to solving mysteries

Traditional approaches to leadership focus on power, influence, and position as the sources of leadership. No doubt, these are important factors in all types of leadership. However, they prove less important in a complex and dynamic world where disruptive change is considered normal. Leaders working in the world of "big data" engage learning rather than power, knowledge rather than influence, expertise rather

Table 2 **Characteristics of a complex leadership environment**

Characteristic	Definition
An uncertain, dynamic environment	Change is rapid, and few situational variables are absolutely clear.
Many different sources of information	Many data streams exist, both internal and external.
Shifting, ill-defined, or competing goals	Goals change rapidly, and there is little agreement about task or process clarity and desired outcomes. Goals may conflict with other priorities and goals.
Need to respond to rapidly changing situation	Situational variables change rapidly and must be accurately identified and addressed.
Ill-structured problems	There is little agreement around the nature of the problem.
Intermittent stress and routine	Periods of high stress are interspersed with moderate or low stress; routine is irregular.
High stakes	The consequence of error is great.
Complex human interaction with machines	Technology is intricate and necessary for job completion.
Multiple players with different priorities	The purpose of individuals differs from that of the group.
A strong culture and code of beliefs	The shared set of beliefs, values, and assumptions are clear and explicitly stated.

Source: Based on Reason, 1995.

than position. Learning-directed leaders see continual learning as their primary advantage, not the hoarding of power and resources. At their core, learning-directed leaders work to be open to new information and ready to revise past assessments of a situation (Mills, 1967). Learning-directed leaders cultivate learning, knowledge, and expertise.

Today's leaders shift their focus from solving puzzles to solving mysteries, as Gregory Treverton (2003) stated in his analysis of policy decisions. Treverton's distinction is a helpful one, but we prefer to use a different language that comes from the study of knowledge and focuses on the structure of the problems and how these problems are solved. The study of knowledge distinguishes between ill-structured and well-structured problems. Well-structured problems, what Treverton calls puzzles, require time, patience, and persistence. Given enough time and resources, leaders can always solve well-structured problems. An example of a well -structured problem is reducing a budget by 15 percent. On the other hand, determining a new strategic direction in a fast changing marketplace is an ill-structured problem. Well-structured problems are the work of traditional leaders. Learning-directed leaders, on the other hand, work to solve ill-structured problems, which look more like mysteries. No matter how much time, persistence, and patience a leader puts into solving an ill-structured problem, it can never be fully understood and people will never fully agree on one right decision. In fact, there is no single best solution for an ill-structured problem. We discuss ill-structured problems in more detail in Chapter 4 and offer strategies for solving them; for now, Figure 4 represents the shift in thinking required for a leader to be successful.

There is some irony that the group that struggles with the notion of ill-structured problems are academics and teachers, the very group we have entrusted to learning! Psychologist Robert Sternberg (Sternberg et al., 2000) describes how our education system fails to prepare leaders for contemporary challenges because of the emphasis on academic rather than practical problems. Educators structure academic problems so that they are well-defined, formulated by the teachers themselves rather than the students. Further, academic problems tend to offer only one or a limited number of correct answers and a limited number of methods for achieving the correct answer. In contrast, practical problems, the kinds of problems faced by leaders outside the classroom, appear to leaders as unformulated, with multiple possible correct answers. Most importantly, practical problems are embedded in everyday experience and often require experience to find a satisfactory answer. In the end, our leaders may be better prepared for solving academic problems than real-world problems, and that in itself is a problem.

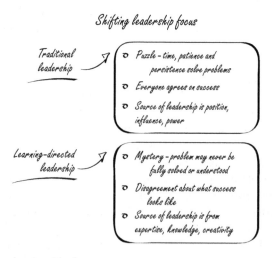

Figure 4 **Shifting leadership focus**

Learning-directed leadership in organizations

The work of learning-directed leadership lies solidly in the world of ill-structured problems. Yet, even with routine work, learning is essential, as an example from the medical profession illustrates.

ELIMINATING INFECTIONS IN CRITICAL CARE MEDICINE

Medical personnel insert or replace thousands of central line catheters each day. These catheters, which are inserted into veins in the neck, groin, or chest, dispense medications or fluids and can be used to measure blood volume. In the most trying cases, a central line catheter can save a life or limit pain. Although inserting one of these devices is a common procedure, every year an estimated 80,000 patients contract an infection that could have been avoided. Between 30,000 and 50,000 of these patients die as a result (Landro, 2010). Despite the routine or perhaps because of it, improving the process of inserting or changing central line catheters has proven particularly challenging. Several factors contribute to the problem. A medical professional may care for hundreds of patients a month. The human mind is only capable of remembering a limited amount of data at any one time, and so keeping track of each procedure becomes difficult. Further, many professionals don't have direct access to the correct supplies. Changing a catheter may prove a challenge because resources come from different locations and quality is difficult to assess. Adding to the problem, changing and inserting a catheter requires coordination among various professionals.

A group of physicians sought to change the way medical professionals go about inserting and changing catheters in patients in order to decrease the high rate of infection and death. Led by Dr. Peter Pronovost of the Department of Anesthesiology and Critical Care Medicine at The Johns Hopkins Hospital, they tackled the problem by turning learning into action (Berenholtz et al., 2004; Pronovost et al., 2006; Pronovost and Vohr, 2010). They began by reviewing prior research on catheter-related infections and related topics. From this research they identified five practices that showed promise in limiting infection. First, they introduced an educational program to teach physicians, residents (physicians in training), nurses, and other medical professionals about the existing procedures and how small changes might reduce infections. Second, they created a central cart that included all the materials needed to conduct the procedure with a greater degree of safety. In the past, medical personnel might have to search for the proper equipment, losing valuable time and focus in the process. Third, they instituted a daily-care plan meeting that addressed whether patients needed a new catheter. Fourth, and most important, they implemented a checklist procedure, adopted from preflight checklists used by airline flight crews. The bedside nurse led the process that ensured the personnel followed proper and safe procedures. The checklist was to be used each time a new catheter was inserted or rewired. Fifth, they called on nurses to stop the process if any care provider failed to follow guidelines, as stated on the checklist. The steps on the checklist were not difficult; they were clear and concise. When inserting a catheter, the professionals were to wash their hands; clean the patient's skin with a disinfectant called chlorhexidine; wear a cap and gown and use a surgical drape; insert the catheter through parts of the body other than the groin; and remove any unnecessary catheters (Goldstein, 2009).

The physicians achieved a successful result by almost any measure. Researchers estimated that, when adopted in 50 intensive care units in Michigan, the procedure might have prevented 2000 infections, reaching an infection rate of near zero (Landro, 2010). For this and similar work, the chief researcher, Peter Pronovost, received a MacArthur "Genius Award." The introduction of this five-point procedure demonstrates the power of learning in organizations. Drawing on decades of research and practice, including in cockpit flight crews, the physicians adapted the procedures for the unique situation presented by catheter infections.

Adapting a preflight checklist from cockpit management promises to transform the process of catheter safety in hospitals. A significant amount of learning went into developing and implementing the program. Perhaps even more important, the learning continues every day because of the process. The process of inserting and changing central line catheters works because it enhances organizational effectiveness through learning. The process illustrates five fundamental results of learning-directed leadership on organizational effectiveness: increasing awareness of a problem or system, learning from (rather than simply repeating) experience, facilitating behavioral change through coordination, improving judgment of individual employees, and breaking down hierarchy in order to transfer knowledge across levels of the organization. We present each of these in turn.

INCREASING AWARENESS

Like most successful organization-wide learning initiatives, the catheter safety effort began by focusing attention on the general problem. The hospitals that adopted the catheter safety process implemented a training course for the general population and garnered the support of management. Frontline employees, those who were responsible for insertion and replacement of catheters, received additional training that focused on the specific elements of the problem. Increasing awareness stands as the first step in learning by focusing the attention of the entire organization on an otherwise misunderstood or overlooked problem.

LEARNING FROM PAST EXPERIENCE

One reason that the intervention proved so successful was that it relied on a comprehensive review of existing knowledge. The researchers didn't start from scratch; they sifted through years of studies, in multiple fields from medicine to flight crew operations. They identified ways to put these research findings into action. But they went further by culling best practices. They identified what practices were cursory and which were central to success. Much of the success could be attributed to the fact that these techniques had been used before, and only the most successful processes were adopted.

The researchers went beyond use of existing experience; they made gains in applying the model to a new situation. No one could logically accept that a flight crew checklist would be appropriate for a hospital. Importantly, the researchers knew they had to adapt the checklist for their own unique purposes. The process of adaptation cannot be underestimated, for it seems that many best practices in organizations go unused because organizations fail to adapt them to the specific circumstances they face.

FACILITATING BEHAVIOR CHANGE

Importantly, the central line catheter awareness program also involved behavioral change by encouraging medical professionals to consider small changes in how they work. Behavioral components included adoption of a common cart, institution of a checklist to detail critical procedures, and establishing standardized review procedures for each patient.

These changes encourage learning because it helps medical professionals focus on the processes most important to achieving the goal, in this case infection-free catheter insertion. At the same time, the professionals develop a clearer picture of the larger task, seeing how their individual actions fit into the larger treatment plan for the patient. Learning occurs through the constant monitoring of patient treatment as given by other caregivers. Thus, the process engages the best element of goal setting. It helps to simplify a complex process by focusing attention on key aspects of a task while simultaneously allowing for learning about the implications for the larger task. The most important behavioral change may not be the actual medical procedures itself, but the improved coordination that results.

We have known for some time that learning is a collective process rather than only an individual one (Reynolds and Vince, 2004). Yet, the role of coordination in learning is often characterized as mysterious and therefore often overlooked. Perhaps this is because coordination can be difficult to observe and capture. Psychologist Daniel Wegner (Wegner and Wegner, 1995) has taken some of the mystery out of coordinated learning with something he calls transactive memory. His early research was largely confined to laboratory studies. In one study, pairs of individuals who had been in a relationship more than 3 months were better able to recall words than those who were not in these relationships. Over the last few years, however, the notion of transactive memory has been confirmed in dozens of studies in real-world settings. These studies largely confirm Wegner's findings—teamwork matters. The catheter safety program demonstrates transactive memory and its role in learning. Teams that demonstrate transactive memory share three characteristics.

First, team members believe in the *credibility* of the information shared by other members. The catheter safety program appears to increase credibility because it provides a shared template, a common repository, and agreed-upon procedure for documenting knowledge. Essentially, the shared checklist replaces individual memory with a team memory. Credibility increases because the checklist serves as shared and likely more credible source of memory, so that memory is no longer assigned to the more fallible process of individual cognition.

Second, transactive memory involves effectively *coordinating* actions. Coordination means that information moves across and between individuals in a way that contributes to the team's overall performance. The catheter safety program encourages coordination by helping a team establish a common set of procedures that guide action. The development, implementation, and integration of a checklist foster learning because coordination becomes an everyday practice, not an abstraction. Coordination leads to learning because it necessitates an agreed-upon procedure, standardizes routine processes, and creates a template for improving processes.

Third, the catheter safety program common checklist improves coordination among a group of specialized professionals. Organizations manage complexity by distributing labor. Nurses, physicians, and residents each perform a specific duty. This division of labor helps the organization but creates challenges for coordination. Learning occurs when team members understand, respect, and utilize the unique expertise of these diverse roles.

Wegner and his studies of transactive memory reinforce the importance of teamwork in learning. Simply stated, people in close relationships perform better than anonymous individuals. The catheter safety program provides evidence that when learning becomes a daily practice, it improves performance.

IMPROVING JUDGMENT

In addition to creating awareness and making incremental changes to behavior, lessons from catheter safety checklists point to another characteristic of learning in organizations: the importance of improving professional judgment. The checklist implementation process marks an important shift from institutionalizing organization-wide policies to allowing experienced professionals to exercise judgment. For example, the development and implementation of a checklist is not abstract but part of the daily routine of professionals. For sure, the implementation of the change required a coordinated effort at all levels of the organization, including strong support from management, but ultimately, the change occurred at the most direct levels of patient care, not policy. The program success results from the learning that occurs as professionals exercise autonomy and judgment unencumbered by overly burdensome institutional rules.

Improving professional judgment is an important part of learning. Vimla Patel developed a better understanding of how medical professionals make diagnoses. One early study (Patel, Groen, and Frederiksen, 1986) helped establish the role of judgment in diagnosing illness. Patel and colleagues wanted to know if experienced physicians exercised better judgment than novices like medical residents. They found that more experienced physicians saw medical situations in a more holistic and complete way than did residents. In other words, physicians relied on a greater source of data, including patient histories and lifestyle data, to make a diagnosis. In non-routine cases, experts rely on "flexible reasoning" to generate alternatives and "recover from incorrect hypotheses, evaluate alternatives," and develop more meaningful courses of action. The study shows how learning plays a key role in exercising professional judgment. Judgment, and its cousin learning, requires adapting, looking at a broad range of information, challenging and understanding context.

BREAKING DOWN HIERARCHY

The cornerstone of the catheter safety program can be found in the introduction and use of a common checklist. However, from a learning standpoint, the checklist itself serves simply to facilitate a larger psychological purpose. It facilitates the breakdown of traditional organizational and professional hierarchies.

Medicine's adoption of checklists builds on a legacy established by commercial pilots. Studies of numerous air tragedies and near misses have revealed that all too often dysfunctional power dynamics among the flight crews contributed to the disaster. Overly authoritarian cockpit captains ignored the insights and warnings of copilots, leading to a crash or near miss. We address the issue of authoritarianism in more detail in Chapter 7 on team learning, but it deserves some mention here as well. The checklist serves to neutralize traditional forms of power such as rank or profession because authority no longer rests in the rank of individuals but in their knowledge, and this paves the way for learning. Nurses and residents gain the authority to stop a procedure if it doesn't conform to guidelines.

Each of these five processes underscores the importance of learning in improving organizational effectiveness. The initial experiment for catheter safety has been adopted by other hospitals around the US. It stands as a remarkable example of learning in organizations. We can't emphasize enough that the learning from such an effort occurs on two levels. The first level is the learning that occurs from engaging in the process of building the procedure. This includes the learning from (1) background research and data collection, (2) conversations around the process, and (3) development of the procedure. The second level of learning occurs as an outcome of the continued engagement in the process itself. To look at a successful program can tell us something important, but looking at an overt collapse of learning can tell us something else. Next we turn to the case of Lehman Brothers and the introduction of ignorance.

Failure to learn at Lehman Brothers

As one way to understand just how the catheter safety program invokes learning, we can contrast it with an organization that lacks learning. This section focuses on Lehman Brothers, an organization that can even be described as a collapse of learning (that is, lacking learning) because it had, at the time of this writing, the largest bankruptcy in the history of the world, topping an estimated $639 billion in assets (Harris, 2010). Hope Greenfield (2010), the former chief talent officer at the once-mighty global financial services firm, discussed the failure of Lehman in an article in *Leader to Leader.*

Over years, Lehman grew into a rigid culture, where it enforced strict informal rules for behavior. The culture served the company well at times, but the same rigidity also restricted the company's ability to learn and adapt. During the mortgage crisis of 2007, the managers at Lehman needed to assess and change their behavior and respond to the need for new direction. Rather, as Greenfield pointed out, managers "stood in the sidelines waiting to see who was going to take the reins next" and occupied themselves with "finger pointing and blame" (p. 35). The culture did not change behaviors even when the company needed that change to survive.

Lehman found itself plagued by widespread turnover, which resulted in continual loss of talent. The constant turnover and loss of talent meant that professional judgment was constantly under threat. As Greenfield pointed out, managers who tried to exercise their professionalism found themselves sidelined and ostracized, and many eventually left the organization. As a result, the culture at Lehman restricted independent professional judgment in favor of rigid thinking. Learning ultimately became stifled.

Team coordination, another hallmark of learning, is built on a foundation of credibility that allows individual team members the freedom to act. However, in cultures that breed a strong sense of competitiveness among managers, it is difficult, if not impossible, to build credible, trustworthy team members that place the team's interests and welfare above personal interests. This culture, described as "an underdog eat underdog world," comprised managers who prided themselves on their work ethic and fierce competitive spirit rather than good leadership. It was seen as an honor in the organization that employees could work hard and be successful without having a degree from a prestigious university. However, this also created problems because competitive spirit often overshadowed level-headed thinking. The head of Lehman was bound for retirement, and his number two in command was not a likely successor. This dynamic enhanced the spirit of competition, since "any newcomer was regarded as a potential rival and there was smug satisfaction in seeing peers falter" (Greenfield, 2010, p. 34). Although some competition can be a good thing, too much competition can lead to wasted resources, knowledge hording, and lack of cooperation. Eventually, problems go unaddressed because leaders lack the information and perspective necessary to overcome problems.

Lehman Brothers had a strong belief of the firm as a family (Greenfield, 2010). While this is generally a positive attribute—with, for example, the firm rushing to help when an employee faced an ill family member—too much of a family culture means that the hierarchy is rigid and unyielding in decision making. When the firm had only 8000 employees, having only a handful of people at the top making the key decisions may have worked, as these were the handful that Lehman believed really understood the business. By the end of 2008, the firm had grown large and complex, but the hierarchical family decision-making had not changed. In fact, Greenfield recounted that the executive committee, formed to make all the decisions, continued to extend the tradition of a family firm. The executive committee briefly tried to expand its membership, involving more in the decision-making process, but this effort was short-lived and threatened those in power. The rigid culture at Lehman shows that when organizations fail to break down rigid hierarchies, learning and adaptation is its primary victim. Firms like Lehman, which continued to employ rigid decision-making methods despite the need to change and involve more constituents, will find their learning stifled.

Lehman Brothers' ultimate bankruptcy was devastating and stands in sharp contrast to the organizational learning demonstrated by hospitals that adopted the catheter safety procedures. The contrast cannot be overstated: leaders who foster learning in organizations perform better, provide better work environments for employees, and stand a stronger chance of survival in the face of threats or challenges, as the next example confirms.

Empirical studies of the value of learning in consulting firms

Remember Geeta, the recent medical school graduate who sought to expand her career into consulting? She might notice that many of the learning principles at work in the most innovative hospitals also show up in the top consulting firms. As Geeta travels across professional fields, from medicine to consulting and back again, she might notice that learning-directed leadership plays an important role in organizational success. Whether the organization is involved in health care, professional services, or other fields we discuss in this book, learning provides an organization with an advantage.

A recent study not only illustrates how learning improves performance, but also confirms that learning adds to the bottom line. The study involved a professional service firm with over 3000 partners worldwide. Professional service firms serve as a good proving ground for the advantage of learning because they face the kinds of problems commonly faced by knowledge workers. Only partners of the firm and only those who ranked at the very top of the firm based on quality of client relationships, performance in growing the business, and strength in managing the practice were included. Thirty-two of the top-ranked performers met the benchmark as the best of the best. This was no second-class group. On average, the partners billed $2.4 million annually and produced a gross margin of 57 percent.

The study first gauged the behaviors and attitudes of the senior partners using a 360-degree feedback process, with five of the partners' peers, five of their subordinates, and their boss completing a survey. Each partner also completed the survey. The survey sought feedback on 20 different competencies considered important by the organization. One cluster of competencies involved leadership, initiative, and planning. The second cluster included knowledge-based competencies such as pattern recognition, systems thinking, and general knowledge of the job. A third cluster of competencies measured the degree to which senior partners valued learning and the degree to which they facilitated learning in others. Just over a year and half later, the researchers looked at the relationship between the competencies and the partners' performance. Performance was measured using two clear, agreed-upon measures: revenue, or how much money the partners brought into the firm and gross margin, or how well the partner utilized the organization's resources. The study was conducted by Richard Boyatzis (2006), a true pioneer in the study of organizational competencies and one of the original champions of the concept of emotional intelligence. Once the researchers collected this data, they then conducted various analyses on the relationship between these two performance measures and the 20 competencies.

The results resonated with learning-directed leadership. While several competencies showed value for performance, only two correlated significantly with both revenue and gross margin: valuing learning and facilitating learning in others. We estimate that the competency of valuing learning accounted for almost $800,000 in additional revenue. Facilitating learning accounted for an additional $1.6 million! Performance on gross margin was over 10 percent higher for those senior partners who valued learning and facilitated learning. Figure 5 illustrates the relative importance of learning (the bottom two bars on the graph) as displayed by correlations between outcomes and the 20 competencies.

As with any study, this study had limitations; however, it provides evidence of a clear relationship between desired performance outcomes and the value of learning-directed behaviors. The study not only shows the importance of learning in knowledge work, but also provides solid evidence of how important it is for leaders to facilitate learning in others. Consider the nature of a consulting firm. A senior partner may visit a particular consulting site perhaps once a week. Indeed, the senior partners play a key role in developing clients, setting strategy for a project, and managing the consulting group. The real work, however, happens with those junior consultants working at the client site day in and day out. These junior consultants and managers identify new opportunities for business,

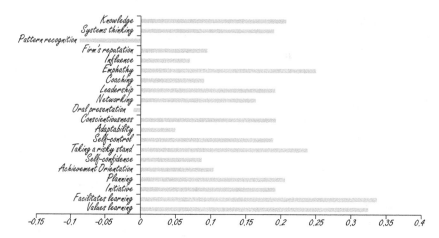

Figure 5 Relative importance of learning compared with other competencies
Source: Boyatzis (2006)

assess client needs, and monitor the daily progress of the project. The junior consultants interact with clients daily, monitor their reactions and moods, and become aware of their demands in a way that senior partners never could. Perhaps most important, the junior consultants learn about new opportunities for business within the client. By placing a strong value on learning and fostering these values in others, senior partners create an environment for learning. Knowledge is gathered, shared, and, most important, used to guide action. Consultants like these highlight the value of learning-directed leadership transforming knowledge into action in the face of ill-structured and novel problems.

Identifying new problems faced by clients, forging new relationships, and building new business lie at the heart of consulting work. Recall the distinction between ill-structured and well-structured problems presented briefly earlier in this chapter. A second consideration for learning involves learning in both the face of complexity and the face of novelty. Figure 6 presents a two-dimensional framework that plots these considerations along two dimensions. Leaders in the medical profession and the consultants share something in common: learning in the face of complexity. For the medical professionals, the situation involved routine. The physicians involved in the effort to decreasing catheter-related infections learned by focusing on the most important issues and standardizing procedures. The consultants, on the other hand, learned to identify novel situations and new business opportunities. The physicians and the consultants both employed learning to improve organizational performance, but learned different things. Of course, the nature of learning is constantly shifting.

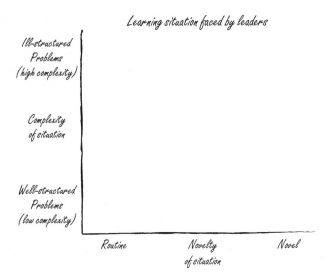

Figure 6 **Learning situations faced by leaders—complexity and novelty**

The consultants will at some point need to learn under routine, just as the medical professionals constantly face novel problems too. We will explore the nature of how learning-directed leaders respond to these situations in later chapters of the book. We conclude this chapter with a specific emphasis on learning and its impact on organizational outcomes, again turning to the medical profession for an illustration.

Learning, leadership, and organization outcomes

A stream of research conducted at the Children's National Medical Center in Washington, DC, further supports the link between leadership, learning, and organizational outcomes. Dr. David Stockwell and his colleagues (2007) instituted a review of the leadership of the intensive care units. They developed a survey called the Physician's Management Index and administered it to 30 residents. The residents ranked the eight attending physicians for the equivalent of 2000 days. The index included 20 items related to leadership and learning such as "acknowledges own mistakes," "manages conflict and stress," "encouraged input from other team members," and "encouraged safe learning environment." Reviewing the results, Stockwell determined that leadership was strongly related to completing daily goals. Only two other factors, age and experience, were even closely associated with performance, but neither were as strongly linked to performance as was leadership. The study shows that leadership is related to experience more than to various environmental factors like the length of rounds or number of patients. The results also show that leadership is learned, as the most experienced leaders were also the best leaders. In summary, Stockwell's research supports the link between leadership skills related to learning and performance, in this case in the form of patient care outcomes.

Conclusion

Through the examples of physicians and consultants we can begin to see how the demands of novelty and complexity shape leadership. The stories of learning in this chapter highlight the remarkable link between leadership, learning, and organizational performance. We provided examples of how expertise, knowledge, and creativity hold a clear advantage over position, influence, and authority. Ultimately, leadership is embedded in learning-directed actions. Despite some of the clear advantages of a learning approach over an authoritarian one, learning all too often is only an afterthought. In many organizations, learning itself becomes a novelty. Even successful cases of learning may be received with skepticism. Despite the growing success of medical management innovations such as the introduction of the Pronovost checklist, many hospitals have yet to adopt the practice. Only the top-performing consultants referenced in one study had adopted learning-directed practices. In our view, too few leaders demonstrate these learning-directed practices. In the next chapter, we look for the foundations of learning and leadership by reviewing key conceptual approaches to learning. We consider learning from a practice-based approach and propose a conceptual foundation for learning-directed leadership in the hope that more leaders will successfully adopt learning-directed practices.

Questions for reflection

1. How important is learning in my organization?
2. What types of complex situations do I face that require learning?
3. What types of learning practices have I encountered in organizations in which I have worked?
4. How can I encourage learning in my organization?

2 Leadership Learning: From the Classroom to the Boardroom

Key ideas

▶ Learning can be classified into four approaches: behavioral, cognitive, social, and humanistic. These approaches offer a broad but often conflicting view about what constitutes learning.

▶ An alternative approach to learning focuses on practices rather than theoretical assumptions.

▶ Drawing on the emerging international field of management learning, we propose a pragmatic approach. Practices of learning are identified that constitute the foundation of learning-directed leadership.

Over the last few decades, a new understanding of how leaders learn has emerged. Systematic research, the latest ideas on leadership learning, and observation of leaders in practice appear to confirm that learning is a key, if often overlooked, factor in successful leadership. This chapter outlines developments in learning that can inform leadership. Although much of what we present in this chapter comes from systematic academic research, we present these ideas using nontechnical terms and try to avoid academic jargon when possible. This chapter paves the way for a deeper understanding of the evolution of learning research and leadership practice that are presented more fully in subsequent chapters.

An understanding of how leaders learn becomes essential for leadership. The emphasis on learning marks a transformation in thinking about leadership. No longer is learning tangential to leadership practice, but learning becomes a central focus of leadership practice. Moving learning from the comfort and predictability of the classroom to the interpersonal frontiers associated with the boardroom is not a simple task. Once accomplished, leaders who integrate learning into every aspect of their leadership will be rewarded with improved performance, satisfaction, and teamwork.

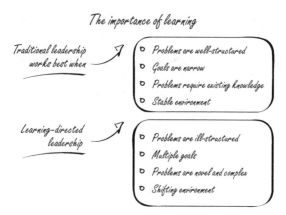

Figure 7 **The importance of learning for leadership**

A leader's story: Leading learning teams in a government agency

Leaders don't often act alone; they often serve as members of a team. One such team, a team of emerging leaders, wanted to identify the benefits and potential challenges to telework in their organization as a leadership development project outside the classroom. They faced some unique challenges because the potential for allowing employees to work out of their home was actively discouraged for many years in their organization. The agency that they worked for managed highly classified documents; in fact, this agency was responsible for maintaining the computer networks over which this information passed. Allowing employees to log in from remote locations, like their homes, promised an almost insurmountable security challenge.

Still, leaders on this team knew that in order to attract and retain the best employees, telecommuting would become essential. The team functioned as an action-learning team for almost a year. Even though the team members worked in locations around the world, their own activity often mirrored the kind of team they wanted to build. They held regular conference calls, shared documents on a dedicated, password protected, website and met "virtually" once a month with an expert facilitator. They reflected on their process, built trust in one another, and developed leadership competencies that would have been difficult to develop simply in a classroom. At the end of the year, they met as a team face-to-face, to compile their learning reflections and propose action steps moving forward to other leaders within the organization.

This action-learning project, sponsored by The Center for Excellence in Public Leadership, represents one of the hundreds of practice-based learning projects working on real problems faced by organizations. The leaders on these teams collaborated. Often times they function without a formal leader, but leadership might rotate among team members over the course of the project. Their goal is not only to solve problems and propose new alternatives for their organization, but also to build learning practices into their work. The telecommuting recommendations of this group resulted in something surprising. One of the organization's key facilities unexpectedly shut down due to a natural disaster. The only solution to keep the network running was to implement the telecommuting plan offered by the team. Not only did these leaders learn valuable skills, but they also improved their organization's productivity.

From the classroom . . .

The study of leaders and how they learn comes from diverse, multidisciplinary research. The cross-disciplinary nature of leadership learning research draws on influences from different fields of study, such as psychology, education, economics, management, critical studies, and sociology. These fields have made important contributions to how we think about leadership learning, but in the end they fall short in providing a practical model for how leaders learn. We propose a new way of thinking about leadership that draws on the best ideas and evaluates their pragmatic relevance to the practice of leadership across many disciplines. To start with, we offer a broad definition of learning. *Learning describes how leaders gather, process, update, and act upon knowledge.* From this general definition, varieties of learning emerge, including behavioral, cognitive, social, and humanistic approaches (Kayes and Kayes, 2007; Bailey and Kayes, 2005).

BEHAVIORAL APPROACH

The behavioral approach focuses on leadership learning as changing or influencing behaviors of leaders and followers (Yukl, 2008). This approach focuses on how external stimuli, of either a positive (reinforcement) or negative (punishment) nature, change behavior. The changes that occur as a result of these stimuli are "conditioned" into the behavior of the individual.

This thinking can be traced back to early theorists such as Pavlov and Skinner. Each contributed to learning by focusing on types of *associative learning*—learning to change behavior by associating behavior with events. The Russian psychologist Ivan Pavlov (1927), made famous by his dogs and their response to stimuli, introduced *classical conditioning*. In his experiments, he could lead dogs to salivate (behavior response) when they would hear a bell ring (stimulus) and receive food. Later the dogs learned to salivate without the presence of the food. This held implications for humans, as humans could also be compelled into a desired behavior with specific stimuli. Controversial Harvard psychologist B. F. Skinner (1969) introduced *operant conditioning,* further expanding on the stimulus and response connection in humans, and described learning as a process where behavior is changed as an uncontrolled response to stimuli. This is an extreme form of behaviorism, in that it limits the impact that thoughts and feelings have on behavior and assumes that behavior will always follow a stimulus in an unthinking manner. Much of the work on rewards and punishments in the workplace relies on the early observations of Pavlov and Skinner.

Despite its influence and seemingly objective and scientific aura, the behavioral approach has been limited by its preoccupation with what can be controlled, measured, and observed. This preoccupation has occurred at the expense of the subjective aspects of learning such as emotions and cognitions. Another limitation is that this approach has relied largely on measuring learning in controlled environments where individuals are not free to choose their own direction without considerable chiding or manipulation. To better understand the nature of the human mind more generally, in contrast to a controlled setting, some have argued that something more than the behavioral approach is needed. The response to the behavioral approach came in the form of cognitive learning.

COGNITIVE APPROACH

Where the behavioral approach concentrates primarily on changes in external, observable behavior, the cognitive approach focuses more on the internal processes or strategies that individual leaders employ to learn, processes that have become known as cognitions. The cognitive approach suggests that learning involves a change in one's thinking, perception, or mental state. That is to say, learning involves not just understanding the visible behavior of individuals, but also acquiring a new understanding of what motivates or directs behavior. The cognitive approach does not ignore behavioral change; rather, it suggests that behavioral change is the outcome of a more complex series of mental processes and strategies and that learning is the investigation into these changing mental processes.

The cognitive approach focuses on different interrelated learning process-es, including selection, storage, and retrieval of information. As such, the dominant metaphor for the cognitive approach is the computer. With a computer, the visible information is only the window to a much more complex set of processes going on inside the computer's processor. Cognitive learning theorists often refer to "maps," models, or "schemas," which are mental pictures held in one's head about the nature of the world. Learning involves changing these maps or schemas based on new information. Thus, the cognitive approach sees learning as the process of changing minds as well as behaviors.

The interest in the cognitive approach continues to grow. While multiple approaches, agendas, and applications of the cognitive approach exist, one of the more interesting manifestations lies in the sensemaking approach (Weick, 1995). Sensemaking describes how interactions between people lead them to make sense of their experiences. Individuals select, impose, and update information in order to function in a complex world. From a sensemaking point of view, learning is about changing how one interacts with others. Learning involves more than just change of mind, however; it involves changing one's identity as well. In some important ways, the sensemaking approach stands in stark contrast to the behaviorist approach. Where the behaviorists see change in terms of discrete, identifiable events, sensemaking researchers view learning as a continual process of adaptation. Sensemaking researchers have a more complex view of what constitutes experience.

It should also be noted that the cognitive approach to learning is not necessarily individualistic. That is to say that, sensemaking, while a cognitive approach to learning, assumes that cognition rests in social interaction, not in the brain of individuals. The social cognition approach, therefore, serves as a bridge between approaches that focus on the individual and those that focus on the social nature of learning.

SOCIAL APPROACH

The social approach focuses on how leaders and followers influence each other. In general, the social approach to management learning suggests that learning occurs by taking in cues and information from the environment. The social approach does not exclude behavioral or cognitive change, but its focus is on the environment in which learning takes place. More importantly, the social approach conceptualizes learning as a function of the social environment in which one seeks to learn. The specific focus may be on the interaction between individuals, extant social norms, or established beliefs and behaviors; however, the process is always social, not simply behavioral or cognitive.

An important distinction between the social and individual approaches, then, is the nature of the interaction as well as the individual's ability to respond to the interaction. For example, the behavioral approach seeks to predict consistent behavior across individuals, regardless of context, while the social approach does not assume this consistency. In contrast, the social approach believes that the specific social context will influence one's behavior. Within the social approach, several sub-agendas exist, including the constructivist and critical approaches.

The constructivists describe learning as a process of creating meaning. An appropriate metaphor for the constructivist approach is making a recognizable figure out of raw clay. The constructivists believe that learning occurs as individuals take raw data (such as language) and construct meaning through it. Constructivists have been heavily influenced by the work of the Russian psychologist Lev Vygotsky (1978). Vygotsky's constructivist approach to learning has been widely integrated into many theories of learning. Most important is Vygotsky's notion of the "zone of proximal development," which he describes as the distance between one's current state of learning and one's potential when working in conjunction with a more experienced other. Constructivists also tend to focus on development, the step-by-step process of attaining higher-order learning. Development has been linked to a variety of management-learning processes, including ethical reasoning (Kohlberg, 1969), interpersonal relationships (Kegan, 1998), career trajectory (Levinson et al., 1978; Levinson and Levinson, 1996; Loevinger, 1976; Schein, 1978), identity at work (Erickson, 1959), and leadership (Heifetz, 1994), as well as overall management success (Jacques, 1989).

Another approach to social learning that is gaining popularity is the notion of "critical learning." A central theme of the critical approach lies in understanding how societal values influence individuals. From this approach, learning looks more like a process of socialization, where individuals learn the cues, rituals, and language of a particular culture or class. The importance of class is not to be overlooked in the critical approach because class determines what is learned and what is not. Although there is a difference in opinion about what it means to be "critical," we might consider three aspects shared by the critical approach in regards to leadership learning.

First, critical management learning approaches challenges the status quo in management education and learning. For example, Dehler, Welsh, and Lewis (2004) challenged the notion of the MBA, suggesting that most management education is itself based on a fundamentally flawed notion of learning. Since the MBA serves as a primary training ground for leaders, they provide a fundamental challenge to leadership training more generally. Second, the critical approach rejects pure rationalism in the learning process. For example, Vince's (1998) noted article drew on power relations and its effect on learning. He took seriously the role of the unconscious. According to Vince, individuals develop psychological defense mechanisms that prevent them from learning. Third, critical approaches see learning as both tied to and stifled by existing social institutions that foster distinctions in social class, norms, power, or coercion. Thus, a better understanding of learning requires a critique and deconstruction of existing social systems, beliefs, and power structures (Reynolds, 1999a, 1999b). A consistent theme that emerges from the critical approach is the notion of emancipation. Emancipation involves becoming freed from the power structures that shackle learning. Emancipation occurs through social changes where traditional social hierarchies, such as class, gender, or even intellectual divides, are bridged through greater understanding.

The contribution of the critical approach to management-learning practice has yet to be realized on a large scale. It may be that many more pragmatically focused organizations find it difficult to accept and put into operation the counterinstitutional values underlying the critical approach. The critical approach to learning asks managers to learn from the social and political aspects of work, not just from experiences with work tasks. The critical approach continues to make inroads into practice and promises to continually challenge dominant beliefs in terms of what constitutes learning.

HUMANIST APPROACH

If the critical approach stands ready to challenge dominant approaches in management learning, the humanist approach stands as its whipping post of choice. This approach focuses on developing the natural human capacity to learn and grow. The humanist approach seems to have moved out of vogue with management learning theorists, despite its continued popularity among those involved in management practice. The alleged fall of the humanist approach from theoretical heights occurred for several reasons. First, humanist values have always sat at the margin of learning, especially in relation to more sobering subjects taught in business schools such as finance and accounting. The fascination with the simple over the complex and the quantitative over the qualitative leaves the humanist approach continually searching for a home among organization studies.

A second challenge to the humanist approach comes from the critical theorists and the growing trend toward social learning. Despite the often-antagonistic relationship between humanism and critical theory, there is evidence that the two approaches actually share much in common. It would be premature, and quite uncritical, to suggest that one can argue for a synthesis of the critical and humanist approaches, yet there is ample evidence to suggest that critical approaches have begun to engage in productive conversation with the humanist approach (see Reynolds and Vince, 2007; Reynolds, 2009).

While the humanist and the critical theorists converse, the conversation is often a fractured one, with a thin but often significant divide (see Kayes, 2002). One reason for the fracturing may lie in the larger cultural contexts under which the two approaches "grew up." The humanists can trace their roots to the human potential movement that emerged in the middle decades of the twentieth century. This movement was closely tied to the group dynamics movement popularized by the National Training Labs. Figures such as F. J. Roethlisberger (see, for example, 1968), D. M. McGregor (1987), and Kurt Lewin (1948) propelled the humanists closer to mainstream management practices. Individuals such as David Kolb (1984) and Bill Torbert (1972) kindled the ideas and forged them into explicit theories of learning. Humanists sought to realize the potential of each individual, a goal perhaps embroiled with the larger cultural theme of American optimism and future orientation. In contrast, the critical approach grew up on the "other side of the pond," so to speak, and sought, either deliberately or not, to challenge this American optimism. Whereas the critical approaches tend to focus on the limits of learning and knowing—in other words, our learning is restricted by our own biases or cognitive and social limitations—the humanists focus on the potential of humans to learn. The humanist tradition tends to be more positive, in that it conceived of human learning as a way to achieve greater actualization for both the individual and society. In contrast to the critical approach, which views human recognition of social systems as the vehicle for change, the humanist movement sees the individual as the vehicle for change. In the humanist view, individuals are limited in their learning only by their own ability or willingness to realize their own potential. Despite their differences, however, both the critical approach and the humanist approach offer learning as a means for leaders to change and grow.

Like the constructivists, the humanists also tend to believe that learning rests in a hierarchical or progressive process of development. Development occurs as individuals become more aware of themselves and move to become actualized in their actions and beliefs. The goal of learning, then, is to reach a position where individuals can exercise considerable control over their own destiny. This, of course, rests in stark contrast to the critical approach, which tends to view the individual as continually constrained by environmental forces.

Lastly, it makes sense to consider positive psychology and its influence on management learning. It is important not to confuse the humanist agenda with that of the emerging approaches on positive psychology (see Snyder and Lopez, 2002) or positive organizational studies (see Cameron, Dutton, and Quinn, 2003). While the positive approaches are not based on management learning per se, they have important implications for management learning. The positive approach suggests that the study and practice of management should focus on positive examples of organizational success (as opposed to organizational failures) as well as on the positive aspects of human psychology. For example, rather than focusing on dysfunction and psychopathology in organizations, managers would learn better by looking at what the organization is doing correctly and how individuals can learn by focusing on strengths rather than weaknesses.

This brief overview of learning serves as the foundation for understanding the various ways that learning is conceived and studied in classrooms across the world. This serves as an introduction to the landscape of learning. In order to fully understand how leaders learn, however, also requires a shift from classroom to boardroom.

To the boardroom . . .

The approaches to learning mentioned in the above section, including the behavioral, cognitive, social, and humanist approaches, provide a foundation for understanding the nature of learning from an academic viewpoint. In this section, we shift the discussion to action and outline learning practices of what leaders actually *do*. We address this question: What is it that leaders do to learn, develop, and improve themselves and others? Learning in a classroom plays a role in leader development; however, learning and its role in everyday practice may prove even more important.

PRACTICE-BASED LEARNING

Building on these more academic-learning theories, an emerging field of research and practice has emerged. Rather than consider learning on primarily a theoretical basis, this emerging approach focuses on practice.

Here the focus shifts the context to practice-based learning or work-based learning. Like the larger study of learning, the practice-based approach is interdisciplinary, meaning that it draws on the learning from many different approaches to leading in order to develop a comprehensive understanding of learning in the workplace.

Few people have contributed as much to our understanding of learning in the workplace as Dr. Joe Raelin at Northeastern University in Boston. Raelin's (1997) approach to learning and workplace practice is reminiscent of Kolb's (1984) experiential learning theory. He bases his notion of workplace learning on the idea that leaders begin with a *conceptualization*, which allows for a questioning of assumptions about their work to emerge. *Experimentation* involves testing assumptions and discovering inconsistencies between ideas in theory and ideas in practice. These inconsistencies can arise from technical, cultural, moral, or personal beliefs. The tacit knowledge gained from the process of experimentation needs *experience* to make sense of this knowledge. Tacit knowledge is knowledge that is contained in a leader's head but is difficult to transfer to others. Finally, *reflection* is the process of thinking about and subsequently surfacing the tacit knowledge to a more specific and conscious knowledge.

ACTION LEARNING

Action learning, long practiced in Asia and Europe, is a method of work-based learning that is growing in popularity (Raelin, 2006; Marquardt, 1999). Action learning involves providing a team with a real organizational problem to solve, having the team learn and at the same time engage in meaningful problem-solving and work. Reg Revans (1982) pioneered the idea of action learning with an emphasis of the collective learning of a group, problem-solving and questioning each other to learn together. Other variants of action learning involve engaging project teams in solving problems. The project team approach often overlooks the collective reflection and testing of assumptions gained through the process of questioning. Although quite popular as a leadership development tool, the learning value varied considerably across organizations based on the methodology that was adopted. Raelin (2006) advocates for action learning because it provides more value at generating real learning experiences than a classroom might, especially when team members are subject to 'stretch' conditions. Stretch conditions might include that the action-learning project involves working in a novel situation or using unfamiliar methods, and that the participants are all committed to the learning experience.

Marquardt (2004) even went so far as to develop specific templates and tools for leaders to adopt with sample questions to make sure that learning occurs in the action-learning project. This helps ensure that the action-learning project is not simply another work project.

Single-loop and double-loop learning

Many leaders that we encounter have ample opportunity to test out their ideas in the workplace, share their knowledge, and refine their leadership

Strategies for leaders

Action learning works because in addition to solving problems and learning from the process of questioning, leaders build personal attributes. Here is a list of common attributes that can be developed from participation or sponsorship of an action-learning project. Select the skills that you might want to work on during the process of action learning:

Leadership attribute	Yes	No
Critical reflection		
Questioning ability		
Willingness to experience change		
Development of personal vision		
Empathy and awareness of others' perspective		
Courage and fearlessness		
Presentation ability		
Facilitation and coaching skills		
Self-awareness		
Team leadership		
Communication		
Humility		
Visibility		

skills. But this testing in the workplace comes with a fair amount of risk that often prevents leaders from really trying out new skills, even with encouragement. Risk is anxiety provoking, and anxiety prevents learning behaviors. Often leaders will be intent on following organizational rules, written and unwritten, saving "face" and maintaining power structures at the expense of learning, especially when learning might involve failure.

The anxieties, fears, and risks associated with learning in the workplace often create roadblocks to learning. Leaders who can overcome these roadblocks can build learning into every aspect of their organization and can transform their organizations into learning entities in themselves. Organizations that learn are intent on becoming more adaptive, more flexible, and ultimately more prone to change and transformation. These types of organizations are effective at seeking out knowledge, making sense of this knowledge, and generating new knowledge. Argyris and Schon (1978) describe organizations as being more productive or less productive at learning. They termed this description of learning as single-loop and double-loop learning. Single-loop learning involves identifying expected outcomes and changing behavioral patterns to obtain these outcomes. Double loop, on the other hand, is about questioning the expected outcomes, and questioning any values, assumptions, patterns, or policies that drove the behavior in the organization.

Another important aspect of learning in practice involves the distinction between theories in use versus theories in action, work that Argyris (1980) generated to better explain the difficulty in becoming a true learning organization. Theories in use are mental maps that guide the behavior of practitioners and the organization in general. This is similar to the tacit knowledge that Raelin (1997) speaks of in his model of work-based learning. The mental maps, or espoused theory, are the conventional wisdom or explanations that practitioners discuss and articulate. These do not often match their theories in use, which makes it problematic for organizations to move to double-loop learning. Using critical reflection in organizations, identifying areas where theories in use do not match espoused theory, allow for new patterns of learning and behavior.

In some cases, an individual's learning may actually decrease the learning of another. Organizational learning is compromised even as the leader learns. Ultimately, the leader seeks to move beyond his or her own learning and improve learning and performance in the larger organization or community. Some of the ideas surrounding organizational learning help us to better understand how learning serves as a tool for leadership and how one person's learning can lead to problems for another person. Anita Tucker and Amy Edmondson (2003) described a situation when learning for one individual might actually lead to problems. They studied how nurses went about solving problems, learning, and addressing errors in hospitals. What

Strategies for leaders

Facilitating double loop learning in organizations involves building the capacity in people to question their own decision-making patterns, the assumptions that led to those patterns and identifying more effective behaviors. This means that as a leader you will need to move from a directive form of guiding people through this process to a less directive approach, where people learn to think and discover these patterns on their own. Here are three stages of *learning facilitation* in the workplace. This learning facilitation can occur informally, when you interact with people on a daily basis in their work or this facilitation could occur during a more formal session, such as on an action-learning team, a project team or other initiative. Your objective is to strategize and practice how you might move to a less directive approach and allow space for people to discover their potential to reflect and learn. You can also reflect on "what are the strengths and limitations of each type of learning facilitation?"

1. *Hierarchical*: In this stage of learning facilitation, the leader directs the questioning of assumptions, and points out habits and patterns that may have led to workplace behaviors. The leader encourages clarification and questioning of other team members. The leader is in the role of "instructor" and is the primary driver of the conditions surrounding the learning process.
2. *Cooperative*: In this stage of learning facilitation, the leader shares responsibility in questioning and directing the learning process. Team members no longer rely on the leader to always ask questions and test decision-making logic, but frequently will question assumptions by themselves. The leader and the team share accountability for the conditions surrounding the learning process. The leader functions in the role of "coach," intervening when necessary.
3. *Autonomous*: In this stage of learning facilitation, the leader has moved into the role of "mentor." This means that the leader is available for support and assistance when asked but that the employees are independently engaged in learning. They routinely will ask tough questions and seek out the answers for them. They are able to identify faulty reasoning and conclusions and revise their decision-making processes where necessary.

(Adapted from Marquardt, 1999)

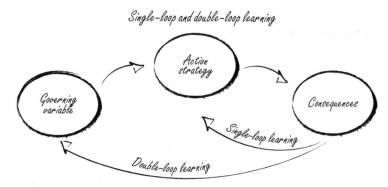

Single-loop and double-loop learning

Figure 8 **Single- and double-loop learning**

they found was instructive for leaders in all kinds of organizations. Nurses, by training, focus on providing strong customer care. Few nurses focus on larger problems in the hospital unless they directly and immediately improve customer care. For example, in one unit, a nurse failed to find fresh linens in the specified linen room. A patient's bed was in need of a change, so the nurse secured linens from another location. In doing so, he was able to solve his immediate problem. The solution required learning as the nurse needed to solve an immediate problem using knowledge of the situation. The problem for the hospital was not solved, however. By taking the linens from the alternate location, the nurse was creating another problem: the night shift would now be short one set of linens.

In the larger purpose of a hospital, the case of the missing linens is of relatively little consequence, but it demonstrates one of the problems with learning. Oftentimes learning only addresses the immediate problem. By addressing the immediate problem we are still left with larger problems and issues. In fact, engaging in learning and solving problems may actually create new problems. Leaders need tools and models to overcome these organizational barriers to learning

Learning in action, practice-based learning, and organizational learning provide tools for leaders to learn, to challenge existing business practices, and to generate knowledge in a more productive way than a classroom can offer.

Learning beyond the classroom

Even a growing number of academic institutions are beginning to understand the limits of "classroom" learning. Work-based learning includes specific forms of learning and leadership, providing internships, field placements, and service-learning projects for students, taking the students out of the classroom and allowing for them to build skills and experience in a work-based or field setting. For leaders it includes some traditional methods such as apprenticeship (learning from a "master"), job rotation (changing jobs), job enlargement (expanding your job), job enrichment (adding more responsibility) and more recently, action learning.

One of the authors, Anna, regularly integrates practice-based learning into her classroom. One class took a group of developing leaders and moved the central class activity from an academic exercise to a community-based, problem-solving event. This activity integrated a combination of practice-based learning and action learning. Since the leaders came from different organizations and wanted to test out their leadership learning competencies in a new and non-threatening environment, a not-for-profit organization was identified that was eager for these leaders to help them. The organization was founded on a mission of social justice and leadership development for disadvantaged youth. Taking the youth and mentoring them, and involving them in justice advocacy in their community, the organization hoped to transform the youth and their communities. The problem that this team of leaders tackled was how to find additional resources for this organization so that they could continue their work. Over the course of about eight weeks, the team worked directly with the organization, increasing their visibility on social media sites and attending and promoting events spotlighting the organization's results. One of the most significant development opportunities was one long rainy day where the leaders walked through a section of the city with the youth and helped them engage in conversations with community business owners. These conversations were learning conversations designed to introduce the youth to the common problems in the community and give the youth a chance to get involved in the change process. The leaders from Anna's class mentored them and participated in the conversations. It was a rewarding learning opportunity for the leaders, the youth, and the organization. Work-based learning served the needs of both those in the organization and the learners. Each encounter facilitated conversation and this lead to improved learning. This set of conversations was key to ensuring that the learning experience was maximized, that is it was not a simple volunteer activity.

Conclusion

By moving learning from the classroom to the boardroom, leaders can begin to tackle many organizational challenges and reach desired possibilities. Learning helps leaders to initiate change, adapt to new and shifting circumstances, innovate, create, solve problems, improve safety, and institute continuity in the face of upheaval.

Our aim is pragmatic. We hope to help leaders adopt learning practices that make a difference in their organizations. Building on the theoretical and practice-based foundations outlined in this chapter, we believe that the following chapters serve as a next step in thinking about leadership. By looking at how leaders engage learning, we can see how learning theory informs everyday practice. By reviewing research on learning and observing leaders in practice, we have identified six practices of leadership learning. The six practices provide the basis for understanding leadership from a learning point of view. That is to say, these practices have emerged primarily as a way to describe the particular experiences, circumstances, or examples of managers and leaders working in organizations. The following chapters illustrate these six practices and offer tips for leaders interested in integrating them into their leadership routine. By moving leadership learning metaphorically from classroom to boardroom, we hope to explain how leaders actually learn themselves and develop learning in their followers.

Questions for reflection

1. Which development in the study of learning do I want to apply in my organization?
2. How do I think people learn best?
3. Does my organization use single-loop or double-loop learning?
4. What are ways that I can develop learning in my followers?

3 Learning from Experience

Key ideas

▶ Learning-directed leaders draw on their own experiences and the experiences of others as the basis for learning.
▶ Leaders have unique learning preferences that impact how they interact and make decisions at work.
▶ Learning from experience involves four interrelated processes: gathering experience, reflecting on the experience, generating theories about the experience, and taking action.
▶ Learning-directed leaders overcome limitations of learning from experience by understanding the structure of the brain and psychological defense mechanisms, their own unique preferences for learning, and the role of anxiety in learning.

Learning-directed leadership begins with an understanding of the learning process and an appreciation for the unique and diverse ways that people learn. Learning-directed leadership suggests that learning can emerge in many different ways. For sure, learning takes place in traditional classrooms, but learning that matters most to leaders occurs when they reflect on their own experiences, particularly their failures and challenges, formulate new strategies for moving forward, and then take a chance in their practice. We begin with a story of publisher Steve Forbes and how he drew on his experience and the collected experiences of his organization to navigate changes in the publishing industry.

A leader's story: Steve Forbes' navigation of changes in publishing

Steve Forbes serves as the Chairman of a media company that includes the well-known *Forbes* magazine of which he is Editor-in-Chief. Run by the Forbes family for three generations, the Forbes empire has developed a reputation for delivering high-impact news to high-net-worth readers, as exemplified in the magazine's annual ranking of the Forbes' 400, a list of the richest people in the U.S. Despite continuity in ownership, Forbes has experienced significant changes in the media business over the last two decades.

In the early part of the twenty-first century, the print media business found itself in turmoil. Memories of the dot-com bust of 2001, during which scores of Internet companies failed, still lingered. Companies had poured money into their Internet sites but never saw returns, and the Internet began to seem like a bottomless pit. Conventional wisdom held that a media company couldn't make money on the Internet, according to Steve Forbes. Despite the growing turbulence and continued skepticism in the online publishing world, a few firms continued to invest in their online business, and by the middle of the decade, the amount and quality of content on Internet sites began to explode. For those who were learning their way around this new medium, a new business model began to emerge.

It is unlikely that Forbes' grandfather and founder of the media empire, B. C. Forbes, could have predicted these dramatic shifts; however, successfully navigating today's environment doesn't require foresight as much as it requires learning. One of the ways Forbes has maintained prominence, while other media giants have fallen into financial straits, is related to learning and especially the ability of its leadership team to learn from failure and cautiously celebrate their success.

In the mid 1990s the World Wide Web held significant business promise. Firms struggled to find ways to make money off what little content existed and many media firms remained reluctant to get involved at all. Those that did simply posted the same content as appeared in print, as many still do to this day. Forbes had a different idea. And because it went against the trend, the firm prospered in both print and online.

"Many people thought that you could just take the written page and post it on the web, and you'd be in the electronic media business," observed Steve Forbes in our interview with him. "We learned early on what Thomas Edison realized about movie production, that a feature film is different from a stage play, that they were, in fact, different mediums altogether." From the start Forbes established the Forbes.com website as a different entity; it was in a separate building and had a different reporting staff and an independent editorial structure. "We knew that print would try to twist the web for its own purpose," he said.

Currently, Forbes.com provides some of the most comprehensive business-related content available. The content includes lifestyle information (such as a list of the best dessert wines) and celebrity watching (such as which stars made the most money last year), as well as a section that discusses the philosophical nature of leadership. Its most notable

feature is a section devoted exclusively to women and leadership—
something that no other major media outlet has.

Even with continued growth and profitability from the Internet side of
the business, Forbes was ready to adapt again. In late 2009, in the face of
declining ad revenues throughout the industry, Forbes pushed forward
on another set of changes. The Forbes management team identified a
need to merge the online and print editorial teams and to engage more
outside resources in content gathering. Despite his successes in taking the
decades-old business into the Internet age, Forbes faced the inevitable
setbacks of an entrepreneur over the years. These setbacks formed the
basis for his learning. Forbes counted some of his failures among his best
learning experiences. A number of ventures, including a news magazine
called *Egg* and the launching of a weekly newspaper chain, never quite
caught on with readers. In the 1990s he ventured into Europe with *Forbes
Global*, a move that reflected a misreading of that market at the time.
"We didn't have a full grasp of the European business culture and what
European readers looked for in a magazine," he noted of the now defunct
venture.

These experiences and his ability to learn from them helped Steve Forbes
lead his media empire into a new era of publishing. He is illustrative of the
kind of leader who learns from his experience yet remains skeptical of it.

> You learn more when things don't go right than when they succeed
> because you start reflecting on the whys and wherefores. However,
> success is oftentimes more difficult to deal with than failure, because
> when you succeed, you begin to think you know what you're doing.

Leaders like Steve Forbes rely on experience as one source of honing
their leadership skills. In this chapter we present frameworks that describe
how leaders draw from their experiences to learn and lead. Learning
from experience means drawing on past experience, reflecting upon that
experience, and testing out new assumptions. Learning from experience
also involves disseminating the new knowledge throughout the organization so others can learn from the leader's experience. The chapter identifies
some of the challenges that emerge as leaders learn. We begin by presenting
a description of how leaders learn from experience.

Learning from experience

The notion of learning from experience challenges some of our deeply held
beliefs about what it means to learn. Learning doesn't just happen in a

classroom, although certainly some learning occurs in a highly controlled environment like a classroom. Neither is learning simply a process of developing a specific skill, achieving a goal, or meeting an outcome. Rather, learning involves a process of drawing on experience to solve problems, adapt to change, and improve performance. Most importantly, learning doesn't occur as a simple process of reward and punishment; rather, learning involves deliberate focus and drive on the part of the learning-directed leader.

THE DEVELOPMENT OF THIS APPROACH: BOTH REVIVAL AND REVOLUTION

In the late 1970s, David Kolb, then a young professor of management at the Massachusetts Institute of Technology, sought a new way to run his classroom. Kolb had been influenced by some of the innovative approaches to learning that had emerged in the past few years. These fresh approaches shifted the center of learning from the knowledge held by the professor to the knowledge held by the students themselves. Kolb, like many of his colleagues, believed that the most powerful learning came from experience, not simply from memorizing concepts or hearing lectures. At the time, however, no one had sought a comprehensive explanation for how people learn from their experience. Kolb turned to a prior generation of teachers who faced similar dilemmas. He considered the philosophy of learning and further took into account his own experience as a teacher, educator, and consultant. He then considered all of this in the current thinking of the day. From these factors emerged an approach to learning that continues to be one of the most influential in shaping how leaders learn worldwide.

Kolb's approach to learning could be considered both revival and revolution. He revised the assumptions of pragmatic American philosophers like John Dewey (1938/1997), who believed education should be based as much on experience as on abstract concepts. At the same time, Kolb's approach proved revolutionary because it challenged the dominant position, held by many business school faculty members at the time, which looked down on experience as the source of learning for leaders. One of his most provocative ideas was that successful learning could occur in a self-taught, professorless classroom. Kolb's early experiments received mixed reviews. Michael Reynolds (2009) was an MIT student when Kolb tested his ideas in the classroom. Reynolds recalled that senior faculty looked down on this new approach but students seemed to embrace it as evidenced by the fact that there was more demand for the class than openings, and several new sections were added the following semester. Reynolds himself must have found the class quite inspiring, as he has spent his own career writing about learning and has achieved widespread international recognition for his own formulation and explanation of experiential learning.

Now a professor at Case Western Reserve University in Cleveland, Ohio, Kolb remains one of the leading thinkers on how people learn from experience. Although some consider Kolb's work mainstream, many aspects of his work remain as subversive today as they did over 40 years ago in the professorless classrooms at MIT. With management schools emphasizing standardization, and accrediting bodies advocating narrowly focused learning goals, many continue to challenge Kolb's assertion that experience stands as the basis of knowledge. Kolb's ideas may face challenges in the classroom, but in the day-to-day world of leaders, experience continues to serve as the source of learning. To fully appreciate Kolb's theory of experiential learning, we need to understand how his approach challenges conventional wisdom on what it means to learn.

CHARACTERISTICS OF LEARNING THROUGH EXPERIENCE

Kolb defined learning as the process of creating knowledge by transforming experience (1984, p. 41). The comprehensive approach offered by Kolb outlines six characteristics of learning from experience (pp. 25–38).

First, *learning is a process, not an outcome.* Too often, when we think of learning, we think about sitting in a classroom, memorizing academic content, or even the mild horrors of taking standardized tests like the SAT, GMAT, or an IQ test. It becomes tempting to think that when leaders learn, they must be focused on achieving specific, clearly stated outcomes and a specific predetermined body of knowledge. While goal-directed learning such as this may be an important element in how a leader learns, Kolb had something else in mind. He saw learning as an activity that leaders engage in on a daily basis. In fact, all of us, when we are in the right mindset, can incorporate learning into our daily experiences. Thus, learning occurs by engaging in certain activities and processes, not necessarily by establishing predetermined goals or outcomes.

Rather than focus on specific outcomes, like test scores or a specific skill, learning for leaders occurs primarily through generating new experiences. The second aspect of Kolb's approach is that *experience, not goals, incentives, or outcomes, is the basis of learning.* The idea that learning rests in a process, not simply in outcomes, presses leaders to think of how they learn in a new way. No longer is learning something done simply in response to some reward or punishment; rather, learning is an inspired act, grounded in everyday experience.

Third, learning is a *tension-filled process*. Said another way, learning involves resolving dialectically opposed modes of adaptation. This sounds a little academic, but in reality it is quite a simple concept. This idea suggests that learning is a process of resolving tensions. Let's say a leader is faced with two seemingly equally weighted choices. Either way she chooses, some potentially good things will result, as well as some less desirable consequences. Thus, when leaders learn, it is natural to feel pulled in two or more opposing ways. As we discuss later in this chapter, learning is not always pleasant, but often results from anxiety. It is this anxiety that causes us to grow and push ourselves toward learning and mastery.

Learning is a *holistic and integrative process*. This is the fourth aspect of learning. Yes, learning may be directed toward specific outcomes or goals. After all, some people argue that a leader's job is to define specific goals and help followers achieve these goals. However, accepting such a narrow approach to leadership limits its complex and multifaceted role. This tells us that leaders must adopt a new approach to learning, an approach that is both broad and long term, not narrow and short term. The work of most leaders requires a broader understanding of learning. Learning, we believe, involves developing the entire leader and the entire follower as a person. In this way, learning involves developing multiple dimensions of the leader, including the cognitive, emotional, professional, and even spiritual.

There are reminders of how leaders learn from the outside world. Recall that US president Bill Clinton read a new book almost every night. Sam Walton, founder of the retail giant Wal-Mart, would visit the stores run by his competitors each week. Examples such as these point to Kolb's fifth aspect of learning from experience: *Learning emerges from the interplay between a leader and his environment*. Learning occurs as a leader engages directly with the outside world. Leaders learn as they reach beyond their deeply held assumptions and find experiences that directly challenge these assumptions.

A sixth aspect of learning from experience is that *learning creates new knowledge*. This characteristic may be the single most important characteristic because it suggests that leader learning involves moving beyond current conventions to create new knowledge. Leaders who learn generate new ways of thinking about old problems. Leaders who learn create meaning out of complex situations and help us to move beyond current ways of thinking, working, and leading.

Jump starting the learning process through reflection

Learning-directed leaders understand the power of learning from experience. As we go about our daily lives, we are likely to describe our experiences with a sense of continuity. Events come and go as a continuous series of uninterrupted new experiences. Because our experience is continuous, we are not often likely to stop and reflect on this experience. In order to learn, a leader needs to "interrupt" this continuous flow of events and create time for reflection. In some cases, the interruption may emerge abruptly from an external source, like the 9/11 attacks in the US or a sudden decline in stock share price. In this case, an external event demands our learning. The interruption might also arise from an internal insight due to reflection on the part of the leader. For example, Robert McNamara, the former US Secretary of Defense and one of the strongest advocates for the war in Vietnam, came to the conclusion that he was wrong about the war only after years of reflection as a private citizen.

Learning occurs as we begin to break down the flow of events before us, identify them as meaningful, and place them within a framework of symbolic meaning. Essentially, learning from experience begins when we start paying attention to our experiences. A number of things can happen to jumpstart learning. We might have a deeply emotional or moving experience. The death or illness of a family member or a significant change at work can cause us to reconsider our priorities or the way we do things. When a deep emotional situation causes us to begin learning, *emotional connections* initiate learning. On the other hand, learning might emerge because a leader comes across an idea. *Cognitive connections* occur when leaders have an idea or abstract notion that they want to understand better. In some ways, cognitive learning stands as the opposite of emotional learning. Leaders also may begin learning when they encounter a problem. Encountering a problem can initiate learning as leaders begin to find ways to solve the problem. Because problem solving often involves a process of trial and error, we call this form of learning *active experimentation*.

As we have described, learning can be initiated in leaders in a variety of ways—through an emotional event, by coming into contact with a compelling idea, or by encountering a problem that needs to be solved. Remember that experience comes to us as an ongoing flow of events, and that for learning to begin, we need to break or slow down this flow. One of the most important ways for learning to occur is through *reflective observation*. Reflective observation involves many different but related practices. At its core, reflective observation requires taking a step back and removing ourselves from the ongoing flow of daily life and trying to take stock of

Strategies for leaders: Facilitating reflection in self and others

Reflection is the process of looking back at past experiences, events, or situations with the intent of improving understanding of what occurred in the past. Here are some methods to build the process of reflection into daily practice. Reflection doesn't have to take a lot of time, but it does take practice.

▶ Schedule time each day for reflective activities.
▶ Meet with people about non-time-critical tasks and discuss past events.
▶ Review your day's activities by yourself at a regular time and write down what you learned that day and what you would do differently.
▶ Review your activities in conversation with a friend, partner, or family member.
▶ Practice yoga, meditation, or other relaxation activities that allow space for your reflections.
▶ Practice asking questions that stimulate reflection and listen to the answers and discussion that they generate.

Here are some questions to spark reflection in others:

▶ What do you know about . . . ?
▶ Why did this occur?
▶ How can we find out more about . . . ?
▶ How could this [insert situation or experience] be better?
▶ What other ways can we use this?
▶ What might happen if . . . ?
▶ How is this connected to other experiences?
▶ What do you want to know about.
▶ Why do you think that?
▶ What do you think others should know?
▶ How can we use/apply this?
▶ How might this work?
▶ What do you remember about . . . ?
▶ How is this different from other experiences?

the activity. Reflection is the process of looking back at past experiences, events, or situations with the intent of improving understanding. Reflective observation provides a deliberate way to engage the learning process. That is to say, reflective observation provides one of the most important tools that allow a leader to break out of their existing patterns and begin learning. Reflection serves as a conscious attempt to step back and assess a situation with the intent to learn. Whether the mechanisms for learning arise abruptly or emerge slowly, whether they emerge from internal reflection or external force, learning comes from our experiences.

Leading through experience rather than recipe: The case of leek and potato soup

Several years ago, one of the authors, Chris, decided to improve his cooking ability. Until this moment his culinary skills consisted primarily of pouring a jar of tomato sauce on a pile of cooked noodles. Perhaps he would even add a few meatballs, found in the prepackaged section at the local supermarket. He found inspiration to break out of his old pattern of behavior from a blog he had heard about. The blogger, Julie, documented her experience learning to cook. Julie chronicled her journey as she worked herself through each recipe in the famous but difficult cookbook that brought Julia Child fame: *Mastering the Art of French Cooking*. Many of you will recognize this idea from the book by Julie Powell, *Julie and Julia: My Year of Cooking Dangerously*, or perhaps you saw the movie with the same title. In either case, Chris found the idea inspiring and decided to enlist Julie's approach to learning how to cook. However challenging cooking these dishes may have appeared to Julie, we can assure you, Chris's experience proved more challenging. He only got as far as the recipe for leek and potato soup, the first recipe in the book.

Chris realized quickly, before he even served his first pot of bitter, starchy soup, that learning a skill such as cooking involved more than simply following a recipe. No matter how closely you followed the directions, cooking involved proficiency, a set of skills that went beyond any particular formula. Especially at the highest levels, cooking involved navigating a complex set of variables and exceptions. For example, Chris eventually learned that using a food processor would produce too much starch in the soup; it is better to use a food mill as the recipe suggests. Some leeks contain too much bitterness and this requires the chef to adjust the ratio of potatoes to leeks. For the most part, these variations fail to appear in the written recipe. Good cooking, it turns out, is not just about the recipe, but also requires a skill in how the recipe is put together and interpreted.

This story tells us something about the nature of leadership. In the end, like the recipe for leek and potato soup, without a measured bit of trial and error, judgment and failure, leadership can never be perfected.

Attempts to lead by following a prescribed formula are likely to result in something flat and flavorless at best, or even bitter. Becoming a leader is not about following a recipe; becoming a leader is about learning when to follow the recipe and when the recipe no longer holds true. This learning is based on four processes.

The four stages of learning and learning style preferences

We identified four processes that initiate learning: emotional connection, cognitive connection, active experimentation, and reflective observation. Engaging any of these four processes can begin the exciting and challenging process of learning from experience. These represent four possible ways to initiate experience, but don't necessarily ensure learning. How does learning itself occur? Learning occurs when a leader engages some or all of these four processes in a holistic way. In other words, learning from experience involves four interrelated processes, of emotion, cognition, experimentation, and reflection, as shown in Figure 9.

As Kolb has described, learning involves four distinct modes. Over time, leaders develop a preference for using one mode of learning over others. We call this preference learning style (see Figure 10). Learning preferences develop over a lifetime. They emerge from different factors. A leader may develop a learning style preference based on personal

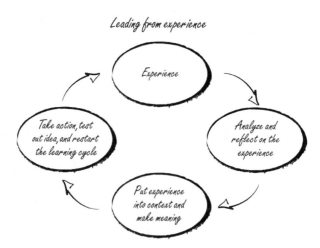

Figure 9 **The learning cycle**

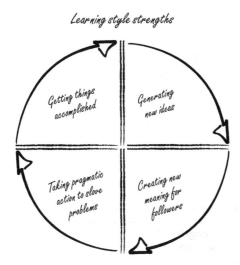

Learning style strengths

Getting things accomplished

Generating new ideas

Taking pragmatic action to slove problems

Creating new meaning for followers

Figure 10 **Learning style preferences**

interests. For example, a leader who likes to engage with other people and develop new ideas may develop a *creating* learning style. A leader may develop a preference due to current job demands and the kind of work performed. For example, an investment analyst may develop a preference for developing and using models or theories. This leader has developed a *planning* learning preference. Training may impact how a leader learns. For example, engineers learn how to solve practical problems using theories. It is likely this type of leader will show a preference for the *problem-solving* learning style. Others may develop a learning style preference for *doing* because their chosen career path of sales requires them to engage with people and close deals.

Each of the four learning styles holds unique skills and abilities in terms of learning. For example, the doing learning style excels at time management, getting things accomplished, and building networks. The creating learning style shines at generating new ideas, looking beyond the ordinary, and building excitement. The planning learning style stands out when it comes to making strong conceptual arguments, making sense of challenging situations, and creating new meaning for followers. The deciding learning style excels at finding solutions to problems, building consensus, and setting realistic time frames for accomplishments.

Taken together, the cycle of learning involves many or most of the activities of leadership. In some cases leaders need to learn by creating; in other situations they need to learn by being logical. In yet other cases they might need to set clear goals or build new coalitions. The notion

Strategies for leaders: Getting unstuck—a new path to learning

Since leaders have preferences in how they learn, it is possible for them to become "stuck" in one mode, without utilizing all of the modes of learning. After all, we tend to enjoy what comes naturally and what we do best, but these preferences might cause us to ignore other ways of learning. The learning cycle involves all of the modes of learning, as each mode has its own strengths that contribute to learning. Table 3 provides strategies to use if you find yourself in a rut or want to help others who are spending too much time in their mode of preference.

Table 3 **Moving from one learning mode to another**

Learning style activity (moving from one mode to the next)	Strengths of the mode	Behaviors that indicate someone is "stuck" in this mode	Questions to move to the next mode
Creating to ...	Generating ideas and possibilities Seeking ideas from others	Doesn't move to *planning* or evaluating the ideas and possibilities in a logical framework Overwhelmed by alternatives	What do others think of my ideas? Which of these ideas have been tried before?
Planning to ...	Making sense of ideas and possibilities Evaluating data Using inductive reasoning	Doesn't move to *problem-solving* or evaluation of frameworks given pragmatic considerations Impractical or complicated ideas	What sense do others make of these data? What explanation accounts for this idea? How does this idea work in a real setting?
Problem solving to ...	Using hypo-deductive reasoning on specific problems	Doesn't move to *doing* or engaging in action on the problem	Which decision is best? What process will we follow? Who is accountable for implementing this idea?
Doing to ... [back to Creating]	Generating action Achieving results	Doesn't move back to *creating*, becoming locked into the same pattern of actions without generating new ideas	Should we try this out or go back to the table and generate more ideas? Is this solution innovative enough or should we come up with other ideas?

Source: Adapted from Kayes, Kayes, Kolb, and Kolb, 2004.

of learning style helps us understand that learning-directed leaders need to develop different and unique skills. Importantly, leadership requires moving through the learning cycle, not getting stuck in any one stage. A leader may develop a particular learning preference, but it is not always best to rely only on one mode or style.

Another factor that may impact learning style is personality. Most researchers and psychologists consider personality as a fixed factor. It doesn't change over time. Even though there may be some flexibility in a leader's personality, over time, our personalities are not expected to change much. Learning style, however, is different from personality. Learning style is meant to be more flexible. In fact, one of the most interesting ideas behind learning style comes from the notion that we can change how we learn.

Learning and the brain

The differences in each of the four stages of learning are not simply academic. Research shows that emotions and cognition actually engage different areas of the brain. Jim Zull, a biology professor at Case Western Reserve University, saw an important connection between the learning cycle and the functioning of the brain. Dr. Zull (2002), who teaches several courses on how the brain learns, drew on his years of experience as a scientist studying science at the cell level to explain the brain's learning mechanisms. He combined his knowledge of biology with his love of teaching and lifelong learning to create a comprehensive picture of learning from the smallest cell to the most abstract of concepts.

As Zull explained, the cycle of learning follows the functions of the brain with remarkable similarity. For example, the sensory cortex, the region of the brain responsible for receiving sensory stimuli from the outside world, mirrors the *concrete experience* function of learning. The integrative cortex, the region of the brain that processes memory functioning through language and spatial and temporal relations, plays an integrative function in the brain. The back integrative cortex plays a role similar to that of *reflective observation* by recall of past experiences, free association, and integration of multiple experiences. The frontal integrative cortex of the brain mirrors the *abstract conceptualization* process of learning. As the language, problem solving, and judgment center, the frontal integrative cortex serves as the coordinating executive function of the brain by bringing all the disparate functions together. Finally, as in the *active experimentation* function of learning, the motor cortex of the brain initiates muscle coordination and translates abstract ideas (hidden brain functions) into observable actions (p. 21).

Zull described how the brain as a learning organism takes in information from the outside world through sensory perception and translates these perceptions into learning through language and various images, memories, and thoughts. Important functions of the brain act in transforming basic data into knowing and connecting the internal world of the mind to the external environment. For example, as we described in the previous paragraph, the back integrative cortex and the front integrative cortex both involve integration of mental work. Yet, these regions often have difficulty communicating with each other. The back cortex works the long-term memory and relies on abstractions such as language and stories, while the front cortex focuses on action, consequences, and responsibilities. In order to understand a situation, therefore, a leader needs to engage completely different parts of the brain in order to make an effective decision. By engaging only the back cortex, a leader is likely to look like a professor, lost in the thought of abstract ideas. By engaging only the front cortex, a leader is likely to look like an overly zealous athlete, focusing only on the present competition with little regard for past or future performances. The very structure of the brain, it turns out, evolved for learning.

The brain structure, however, also poses some important limits on how leaders learn. Without considering these limits, we might be tempted to think that leadership involves simply innate or biological processes of learning rather than intentional social processes. In order for learning to occur, the brain requires deliberate exercise, just like other parts of the body. Leaders need to develop different parts of their brain or they become limited by their own biology. Leaders need to develop the brain in order to meet the changing demands of leadership. True, the brain is a complex organ and involves many interrelated functions. Researchers have only begun to explore the connections between learning and the brain, and our explanation does not do justice to the richness. The important issue for leaders lies in the notion that the learning processes track brain functioning and that learning involves retraining the brain, just as if we were retraining a muscle in the body.

BRAIN PLASTICITY AND THE BRAINS OF RIGHT-HANDED LONDON TAXI DRIVERS

Although its structure may limit what and how we learn, the brain is not fixed in size or capacity but is a living, growing organ. Brain researchers use the term *brain plasticity* to describe the astounding ability of the brain to grow and transform. A study of London taxi drivers provides support for the idea of brain plasticity. London taxi drivers are among the most learned professional drivers in the world. As in many other major cities around the world, London's streets developed in a haphazard way over centuries. The streets are confusing and difficult to navigate. In order to earn the title of professional taxi driver, London taxi drivers must find a pattern among the seeming maze of streets and memorize each street name or else risk failing the dreaded London taxi driver test. What is the test of a London taxi driver? He or she must be able to drive to any street in the city.

A study appeared in the *Proceedings of the National Academy of Sciences of the United States* (Maguire et al., 2000) that detailed the brain images from 16 London taxi drivers and compared them with images of the brains of others who did not drive taxis. Learning and recalling streets and navigation patterns are thought to occur in a section of the brain called the hippocampus. Research with animals has suggested that this region of the brain is associated with memory and navigation skills. More specifically, the back of the hippocampus located on the right side of the brain is associated with the special navigation that would be necessary for success as a London taxi driver. In contrast, the back section of the left hippocampus is thought to be associated with memories of people and events. All the participants in the study, it should be noted, were right-hand dominant. This is important because in left-handed drivers, the brain functions might be reversed. The study found that the section of the hippocampus associated with special memory and navigation was significantly larger in the taxi drivers than in those who did not drive a taxi.

We could stop here and be satisfied that London taxi service was better off because those right-handed individuals with larger right-back hippocampi were finding their way into taxi-driving occupations. Yet something more interesting seems to be driving this phenomenon. The researchers tracked the experience of the taxi drivers in relation to the size of their right-back hippocampi. They found an almost perfect correlation between the increase in size and the number of months learning to be or practicing as a taxi driver. This suggests that the more time on the job, the greater the size of the back hippocampus. In addition, there was a negative relationship between the sizes of the front of the hippocampi in these drivers. The study suggests that indeed, brain plasticity, a change in the structure of the brain, can emerge as a person learns. The authors of the study concluded that brain structure, in some cases, is the result of learning and is not simply genetic. Further, they concluded that the ability to learn new street patterns and navigational routes is a learned behavior, requiring the development of learning specific brain activity as opposed to simple recall of existing information.

The study links the decades-old notion of learning from experience with the most recent brain research. Although further work is still needed and sophisticated brain research is in its infancy, we can begin to see physical evidence that people can learn, change, and even grow based on environmental, occupational, and experiential demands. As the authors of the study concluded, learning itself may involve a complete "rewiring" of the brain so that brain activity shifts from one processing center to another. In this case, the brains of London taxi drivers began by learning new routes in the beginning, as demonstrated by increases in the posterior hippocampus, and then shifted brain activity to storing and retrieving the routes once these routes were established. To say that learning occurred at every street corner may be overstating the case a bit, but it is accurate to say that the drivers did learn every street corner.

Psychological defenses and blocks to organizational learning

Many years ago, one of the authors, Chris, was presenting a model of experiential learning at an academic conference in Canada. His lecture involved defending the notion that learning involved primarily a four-stage cycle and expanding on that model. As part of the lecture, he identified a number of recent faculty who were challenging the model on a conceptual basis. One of the models that Chris had targeted was by Professor Russ Vince. Vince's model suggested that additional factors were at play in learning from experience. It turns out that Professor Vince was in the audience of this lecture. What developed, however, was not a boring academic debate, but rather a highly engaging and fruitful discussion on the nature of learning—a conversation that has ensued between the two for over a decade and that has extended across two continents. The debate between them has emerged in two published collaborations and many fruitful discussions. It is worth spending some time on presenting Professor Vince's (1998) view of experiential learning because it helps us understand some of the challenges that leaders will face when learning. Vince's model helps illustrate and integrate how defense mechanisms can play a part in stifling learning (see Figure 11).

Vince's work emphasizes the role of emotions in learning. Ultimately, he argues that these emotions serve as the basis for all or most learning. Emotions like anxiety, fear, and doubt can serve as either the starting point for learning or its end point. He believes that when leaders learn, they are often unaware of their own emotions and how they are reacting to a particular learning situation (p. 310). Further complicating the situation, many organizations discourage expression of emotions. As a result, these emotions are not allowed to surface, the emotion becomes suppressed,

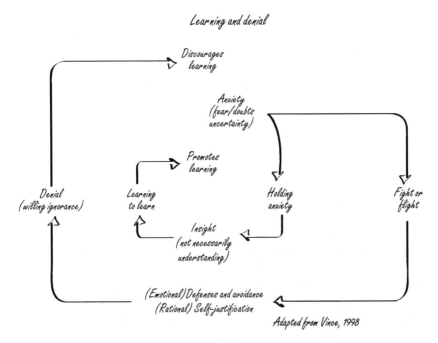

Learning and denial

Figure 11 **The role of psychological defenses in learning**

and learning suffers. Here is Vince's formula in more detail. As he said, the turbulence that these emotions cause within us is characteristic of our need to learn (p. 311). Recognition of these emotions and an environment that allows for the safe expression of these emotions provide an opportunity for deep learning. On the other hand, the anxiety that results can lead to defensiveness, combativeness, outright denial, or rationalizations.

These emotions can either destroy our learning or develop it. As psychologist Edgar Schein (Coutu, 2002a) said, anxiety inhibits learning, but some level of anxiety is also necessary for learning to happen at all. Schein outlined two types of anxiety. *Change anxiety* is fear of trying something new. For example, fear comes from looking stupid, giving up old habits, or criticism. Ashley, a government contractor that we worked with, expressed terror at having to do public speaking, a fear that many people hold. Her fear of public speaking compelled her to avoid almost any situation where she might have to stand up and perform the dreaded task. Ashley often described in detail the imagined criticism that she might receive from her audience. This anxiety caused her to prepare elaborately prior to any event where she would have to speak. Her detailed preparation, research, and painstaking practice paid off over time. Ashley was recognized as an influential leader in her organization. Her anxiety pushed her to new limits that ultimately gave her a professional advantage over others.

Survival anxiety is the kind of fear that we must do something to survive. In survival anxiety, external threats may be the strongest motivator. One leader we spoke with, Tim, an account supervisor, was overcome by fear because he thought he would lose his job if he spoke up in meetings. The culture at his workplace, a financial services firm, paralyzed him from saying anything in a meeting that would make him stand out. Tim was convinced that "speaking" at meetings equated to job demotion and loss. We never spoke with others in Tim's organization but wondered what the perception of him was. We also wondered whether he had confirmatory data for his fears or if they were simply his vulnerabilities manifested, deceiving him and holding him back. Schein made a keen observation in an interview in the *Harvard Business Review* about the importance of learning and leadership: "Unless leaders become learners themselves— unless they can acknowledge their own vulnerabilities and uncertainties, then transformational learning will never take place" (p. 105).

Psychologist Emily Balcetis (2008) indicated that our anxiety could block our learning and result in a form of self-deception. We engage in these self-deceptions to maintain our present belief system, but the real victim of this anxiety is our own learning and our ability to gain a comprehensive understanding of a situation. She summarized four potential consequences that result from our self-deception. First, self-deception involves building barricades and filters in order to select which information a leader sees as relevant. Second, self-deception compels a leader to build firewalls to ward off threats. This allows leaders (and their followers) to maintain a positive sense of self when anxiety or threats to identity began to surface. Third, self-deception means that leaders adapt different measures for accepting and incorporating positive and negative information. Leaders encourage positive information to pass quite easily into their assessments of a situation, whereas they are extremely reluctant to allow negative information to enter into the intelligence mix. As one leader noted, "You rarely get questioned on information that conforms to prevailing thoughts." Fourth, self-deception makes leaders construct their own experiences so that they recollect only those events and attributes that conform to their present identity and that help them imagine the future desired by followers.

Tim could articulate one situation where an account representative had been terminated at work. In Tim's assessment, this account representative was frequently vocal at meetings, and this confirmed Tim's worst fears. When we pressed a bit further, Tim disclosed that this account representative also had the lowest sales volume for the branch compared with other representatives. Remembering this former coworker as someone who was outspoken and was fired, however, conformed to Tim's notion of what would happen to him if he spoke up at meetings. This discrepancy between what is reality and what is belief is similar to differences in what leaders say and what leaders do.

Helping others learn from their experiences

Helping others achieve success is a hallmark of the learning-directed leader. David Hunt (1987), a psychologist, counselor, and executive coach, explained how the learning cycle serves as a process of mutual influence that can help individuals improve how they learn collectively. Hunt described how a person identifies and activates each of the four modes of learning internally and then how each of these four modes becomes activated in another person, externally.

The process occurs in four phases. First, a person identifies how he or she experiences each of the four learning modes. In this step, the leader engages in some self-reflection to better understand his or her learning style. Step two extends step one by helping an individual move beyond individual preferences and experiences to acknowledge how others in the group experience different modes of learning. For example, the leader and a coworker may have a conversation about individual learning styles or how each prefers to enter the learning cycle. The third step requires a more complex process of identifying what kinds of activities, conversations, or interactions motivate an individual to move from one learning mode to another, say from abstract conceptualization to active experimentation. Here the conversation might turn to identifying sources of anxiety or defenses that block learning. The fourth step of this process involves identifying which learning mode of one individual activates which mode in each of the other individuals. Hunt argues that group learning is important because he believes that the interactive relationship between one mode of learning in an individual does not necessarily motivate the same mode in another individual.

Conclusion

This chapter has outlined the importance of learning from experience as a practice for leadership. Understanding the learning process, encouraging others to engage in and navigate the learning cycle, and overcoming psychological anxieties associated with learning are key to learning-directed leadership.

Questions for reflection

1. What is your learning style preference? What unique skills do you have based on your learning style preference?
2. What challenges have you faced engaging the learning cycle? What have you noticed about others and the learning cycle?
3. How have emotions or anxieties impacted your learning? What observations have you made about others and the impact of emotions or anxieties on their learning?
4. What problems might occur with an overreliance on your own experience? What is the best approach to utilizing experience?

4 Higher-Order Learning

Key ideas

▶ When leaders engage in higher-order learning, they experience a continual improvement in their capacity to learn.

▶ Leaders who develop higher-order learning are not limited by their pre-existing experience but learn to transfer their learning to new situations. Learning no longer becomes constrained but can be applied to a variety of situations. Leaders seek out new and unfamiliar situations and continue to learn.

▶ Higher-order learning involves three progressive steps: learning from experience, deliberate practice, and meta-learning.

▶ Stress, multiple competing demands, and emotional burnout conspire to undermine higher-order learning.

Higher-order learning marks a turning point in learning-directed leadership as it is one of the more complex of the leadership practices to master. As leaders adapt to new challenges, the way they learn must adapt as well. Leaders develop the ability to meet new and unexpected challenges by developing higher-order learning. Those who demonstrate higher-order learning are more agile and flexible in their learning and thus are more likely to learn in the face of stress, novelty, and ambiguity. The result of higher-order learning is a consistent focus on relevant information, simultaneously balancing the larger mission with short-term tactics, taking action in the face of ambiguity, and managing multiple, even conflicting goals.

Two military examples help illustrate the nature and importance of higher-order learning in leadership. The chapter begins with the story of an Army Ranger Quick Reaction Force, which engages higher-order learning to capture a strategic mountaintop in Afghanistan. It concludes by mapping General Robert E. Lee's higher-order learning throughout the US Civil War to demonstrate the threats to higher-order learning.

A leader's story: Captain Nate Self and the army rangers in Afghanistan

"Fly to Cardez, land the aircraft, we'll figure it out." That was the extent of the mission. Army Captain Nate Self had only a few fragments of information. Within hours of hearing his mission, 25-year-old Captain Self and his team crouched down in the MH-47 helicopter and faced the uncertainty of their mission. They would likely find themselves landing in the middle of an ongoing operation or, worse, picking up the pieces of a failed mission (Naylor, 2005; MacPherson, 2005).

The situation was volatile, the specific goal shifting. Self and his team would learn the underlying reason for their mission only after hours of fighting. Unlike conventional forces, with their detailed action plans, Self's team constantly shifted its efforts and goals based on incoming information. Even before their helicopter landed, control of the mission had moved from Central Command to Ground Command. The nine men, many still teenagers, carried only light arms (handheld machine guns) so that they could get in and out of a situation quickly—thus the name, Quick Reaction Force. Two Air Force rescue jumpers and an eight-person flight crew guided the mission along with the Quick Reaction Force.

"It seemed to me somebody made a pretty big mistake," Self would later recall (Phillips, 2006). The helicopter carrying the team and crew reached 30 feet above the insertion point at 5:40 a.m., but before the helicopter could land on the cold snowy ground, an RPG, basically a hand-launched missile, exploded into the side of the helicopter. An RPG has a short range, 200–300 feet or so; the enemy was close.

Within seconds the helicopter was taking gun and RPG fire from all sides. Self still held only an incomplete picture of his mission, and the specifics of the situation continued to shift second by second. He began to assess the situation, "How many men have I already lost?" He heard the wounded but could not tally his men. Those who were still alive needed to move fast if any of them were to stay alive. Just as he exited the helicopter, his weapon jammed. His first time in battle tested his ability to adapt (Self, 2008).

Self and his team continued to receive fire as they exited the back of the helicopter. He struggled to gauge the location. Although the fire appeared to come from above and around the helicopter where they took cover, he could not be sure that was the only enemy location. With the helicopter as their main source of cover, Self realized his team was vulnerable. The next move would be to work their way right into the line of enemy fire, finally finding cover near an outcropping of rocks that served as a temporary refuge. After a series of trials, the Quick Reaction Force got through to Joint Special Forces Command, sidestepping both orthodoxy and official protocol; the young Captain Self now reported directly to a two-star general.

Elements of higher-order learning shown in Self and his team

Self and his team had no prior experience in combat. Still they acted not like novices, but more like experts (see Klein, 1999). They fought off the enemy and eventually took control of this 10,000-foot mountain named Takur Ghar, or High Mountain, but the cost was heavy, nine American soldiers died in the battle.

How is it that a leader and his team with no experience in direct combat can function like experts in a novel and complex situation? We believe it is because Captain Self and the Army Ranger Quick Reaction Force displayed a form of what we call higher-order learning. Specifically, the events on Takur Ghar represent the ability of a leader to guide his team through multiple forms of learning simultaneously. A closer look at the events on Takur Ghar in the context of the practice of higher-order learning helps make this connection. At least four types of learning emerged: learning from experience, exploratory learning, counterfactual learning, and evidence-based learning.

LEARNING FROM EXPERIENCE

In Chapter 3, we discussed the importance of learning from experience. In the case of the Army Rangers on Takur Ghar, this learning occurred not from actual experience but from simulated experience through training. Essentially, the teams learned beyond their own immediate experience. Still, experience played an important role in their learning, because it provided the foundation on which new knowledge was gathered and served as the basis for action. It is through experience-based learning that leaders develop basic theories about cause and effect that direct action and inform managerial decisions (Klein, 1999). Experience-based learning involves direct observation of the world and engagement in the ongoing flow of events so that experience, no matter how immediate or short, can guide action. As the basis for all higher-order learning, it was their adaptation and response to immediate changes in their environment that marked higher-order learning.

One form of experiential learning that may have guided action was analysis of prior combat situations and observations of ongoing operations that set the context for the experiences on Takur Ghar. If learning from experience was the only form of learning we noticed on Takur Ghar, then this leadership story could have been reserved for Chapter 3, but the learning on Takur Ghar demonstrates a shift from experience-based learning to higher-order learning.

EXPLORATORY LEARNING

Experiential learning refers to learning from previous experience, while exploratory learning refers to creating new experiences where existing experience falls short. You can think of the learning that the Rangers demonstrated as *exploratory learning*, in that they actively sought to create new sources of experience. Exploratory learning has its basis in a stream of learning research (Schulz and Bonawitz, 2007; Schulz, Goodman, Tenebaum, and Jenkins, 2008) focused on how children use evidence to learn about their environment. Schulz and a team of researchers found that children are remarkably adaptive when it comes to learning abstract principles of cause and effect. Only a few trials were needed for children to develop a reliable model of what actions lead to what events. Interestingly, Schulz's studies revealed that these mental models, imagined maps of how a situation works, were acquired quickly in test subjects but were difficult to break once the cause and effect patterns were established. These beliefs about causes and effects prove difficult to change, even when they were no longer supported by evidence. Although Schulz conducted these studies with children, the findings suggest patterns for leaders too. Leaders may hold on to existing beliefs (in the form of mental models) even after they experience evidence to the contrary.

Shultz found an additional element in her research that tells us something important about higher-order learning. Despite the fact that mental models were formed quickly and were difficult to change, Shultz noticed something interesting about how children began to learn when confronted with data that contradicted their existing beliefs. They were more likely to move into a state of exploration and learning in order to find an explanation to explain the discrepancy. Thus, learning occurred, but only prompted by disconfirming evidence. Higher-order learning involves understanding that mental models only hold in certain situations. Higher-order learning requires challenging pre-existing experience by embracing disconfirming evidence and moving into a practice of exploration.

This began as soon as the Rangers fought their way out of the helicopter and secured the ground around the helicopter. Exploratory learning can be seen in several of their actions: initiating contact with various teams in the area, including SEALs (The US Navy Sea, Air and Land Teams) and a second Ranger Quick Reaction Force in the area; contacting multiple command centers; and reviving their communications equipment through trial and error.

Most notably, Self and his team moved into the practice of exploratory learning as soon as they called for air support. An F-16 fighter jet temporarily suppressed the enemy fire that came from the fortified bunker on the top of Takur Ghar. A second air attack by a B-52 bomber was called off, because its bombs lacked the precision to hit the bunker. The Rangers, at only a few hundred meters away, were at an unsafe distance from the effects of the explosion. A third air attack, flown by a pair of F-15 fighter jets, guided missiles, but these too landed within several hundred feet of the Ranger team. In all, an estimated 30 strikes were carried out on the targeted enemy bunker over a 15-hour period. None of these aircrafts, however, had the precision to destroy the bunker (Headquarters United States Air Force, 2005, p. 77). Exploratory learning, or trial and error learning, attempts to reconfigure cause-and-effect relationships by challenging current experience. It too has limitations. Exploratory learning may only be effective when current circumstances provide immediate feedback.

COUNTERFACTUAL LEARNING

Under some circumstances, learning is best practiced through *counterfactual learning*. Researchers Morris and Moore (2000) observed that counterfactual learning is most appropriate in situations where prior experience isn't instructive because the leader hasn't experienced a particular situation. Said another way, counterfactual learning is most helpful in the face of new situations. Under these conditions, counterfactual learning challenges the consensus view but identifies factors that have low probability of causality. In other words, counterfactual learning improves decision-making when evidence is solid but causal links are unclear.

In Self's case, the use of counterfactual learning seems to have involved asking a series of "what if" statements about possible ways to destroy the enemy bunker: "What if we could get air cover?" "What if we could advance on the bunker?" and "What if we could get a Predator drone to launch a missile on the bunker?" As Self watched the failed attempts at destroying the bunker using air force, he recalled one of his nights at the Command Center and remembered that some of the Predator unmanned vehicles carried guided missiles. He communicated his intention to the General. He asked if one could be used to hit the bunker. The military did not operate any Predators that carried the guided missiles, and no

protocol or precedent existed to use an armed Predator in combat. The
Predator was the property of the US Central Intelligence Agency, not
the US military. In the end, the Predator attack destroyed the enemy
bunker on the mountaintop, allowing Self and his team to complete their
unstated original mission: to recover the body of fallen Navy SEAL Neal
Roberts who was killed in a failed attempt to take the mountain that
was launched less than 12 hours before. In recovering the body, Self and
his team were also able to take control of the mountaintop from enemy
forces. Captain Nate Self, and his use of experiential, exploratory and
counterfactual learning, illustrates how leaders practice multiple forms of
learning, often at the same time.

To clarify the process by which leaders achieve higher-order learning,
we turn to emerging streams of research in the areas of learning, adult
development, and expertise (see Figure 12). Higher-order learning, like
that demonstrated on Takur Ghar, is the result of three interrelated learning
practices: learning from experience, deliberate practice, and meta-learning.
Leaders who develop higher-order learning are not limited by their pre-
existing experience but learn to transfer their learning to new situations or
to seek out new experience. Learning no longer becomes constrained to
specific situations but can be applied to a variety of situations with similar
characteristics. Despite competing pressures and commitments, these leaders
seek out new and unfamiliar situations and continue to learn. Oftentimes
stress, multiple competing demands, and emotional burnout conspire to
undermine higher-order learning, but ultimately higher-order learning can
prevail as leaders engage multiple forms of learning and continually reframe
existing mental models.

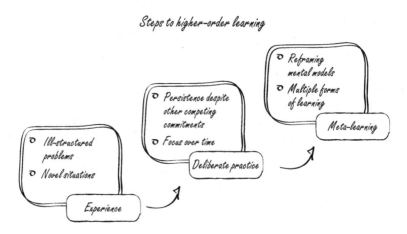

Figure 12 **Higher-order learning**

At its core, higher-order learning involves understanding one's own learning and one's own ability to learn in multiple ways depending on the situation. Learning in this capacity takes time.

Improving leaders' capacity to learn over time

Higher-order learning isn't just for military leaders. CEOs of top American and European companies such as IKEA, Nokia, and H&M demonstrate higher-order learning when making their toughest decisions. Top leaders refrain from choosing between conflicting outcomes such as long-term strategy or short-term performance drivers. These learning-directed leaders don't see their role as simplifying complex and paradoxical situations. Rather, many top leaders explain that their role in the organization is to keep complexity and paradox while simultaneously allowing for action. Rather than choosing between two options, they try to make multiple, even contradictory, things happen simultaneously (Fredberg, Beer, Eisenstat, Foote, and Norrgren, 2008).

Strategies for leaders

Leaders have access to several tools to improve higher-order learning. Remember, you must move beyond drawing on your own experience to move to higher-order learning.

▶ Seek out the experiences of others who view the world differently, who come from a different background, who have a different personality or skill sets.
▶ Face new situations with an open mind.
▶ Create opportunities and time for reflection. Examining experiences allows you to synthesize different perspectives and approaches.
▶ Engage in conversation with others about novel situations and unstructured problems with the goal of listening to someone else's perspective and learning together how to approach it. This requires thinking differently, as many conversations are not designed for learning but are designed to convince someone of your beliefs and ideas.

How these CEOs and other leaders develop higher-order learning is a fundamental question of leadership. In theory, at least, a leader should develop higher-order learning simply from experience. Leaders develop through "stages" over time and develop mechanisms to function in new and challenging environments. Each stage presents new challenges for the leader. In turn, the leader responds by finding novel ways to overcome the challenges.

Over the years, observers have applied higher-order learning to a variety of leadership situations. Harry Levinson (1976) focused on how learning changed with a leader's career stage. He tracked leaders' major dilemmas from their first job through retirement. He believed that each new career stage required new ways of thinking, leading, and managing. Groundbreaking psychologist Eric Erikson (Gale, 2001) focused on life stage and the particular demands faced by individuals as they moved from young adulthood to old age. Yet another model, often referred to by the name of its creator, Bloom's (1956) taxonomy focused on how students comprehend material and gain knowledge as they progress through stages in their education. Jean Piaget (2001) put forth perhaps one of the most influential models of development. Piaget observed his own children and their playmates as they matured from infants to toddlers to young children. He concluded that at each stage children processed information differently.

One approach to explain a leader's learning progression that we have found particularly helpful is the Stages of Contribution framework provided by the Novations Group based on the work of Gene Dalton and Paul Thompson (1993). According to the model, individuals move through four distinct but overlapping stages as they develop as a leader. In stage 1, leaders serve as *dependent contributors*. Individual leadership contributions are expressed through technical skills or job-specific know-how. As is often the case when starting out, dependent contributors act as leaders primarily by carrying out the strategies of others. In the second stage, *independent contribution*, leaders begin to have discretion over their individual tasks. They often set their own agenda, but their leadership contribution remains largely individual. The third stage represents an important shift, where leaders begin *contribution to the organization through others*. Like the two previous stages, the third stage requires a new set of skills. Since leaders now need to rely on others to accomplish leadership goals, they must gain new skills related to influencing, motivating, and delegating to others. Leaders with an interest in building the skills necessary for contribution through others can refer to the emotional intelligence skills discussed in Chapter 6. Finally, leaders may move to the fourth stage of contribution—*contributing strategically*. In this stage leaders must consider the entire strategic direction of the organization as well as the larger context in which the organization works (see Novations Group, 2004).

The distinct, but related approaches to higher-order learning offered by Novations, Piaget, and others describe how leaders move from lower to higher levels of development. The Novations Group, though, was interested in leadership, learning, and career stage. Despite the diversity of approaches to development, no single model provides a comprehensive answer to address leadership in its totality. While these developmental approaches may disagree about the specific nature of development and its motivation, all approaches agree that learning changes over time and that each new stage of development requires leaders to respond to new challenges by acquiring new skills. These new challenges cannot be solved with simple answers and linear thinking alone.

From ill-structured problems to world construction

Leaders begin to engage in higher-order learning when they leave the world of linear thinking and take on the world of ill-structured problems. Researchers have known for years that intelligence per se plays an important, if limited, role in leadership. Performance on standardized tests like the IQ test or college entrance examinations such as the SAT, GMAT, or GRE shows some, but inconsistent, results in predicting future leadership success. Summaries of research suggest that standard intelligence can account for only about 25 percent of career success (e.g., Sternberg, et al., 2000). Although intelligence has some potential as a predictor of leadership potential, many have concluded that it only serves as a baseline for leadership. Said in common terms, some minimum ability in intelligence is necessary but it doesn't predict leadership effectiveness. Because of the limited value of intelligence in predicting successful leadership, another alternative looks at a leader's ability to learn and how this learning changes, and in fact improves, over time.

In contrast to the worldview that the workplace is a simple series of linear and well-defined problems, a leader's work is more complex. The workplace for leaders is oftentimes the world of ill-structured problems and trade-offs. Leadership success is defined by how a leader approaches the nature of tasks at work, the complexity of the environment, and the complexity of the thinking that goes into solving problems. King and Kitchener (1994) offer a valuable description of these types of ill-structured problems faced by leaders in their model of reflective judgment. They describe three characteristics of ill-structured problems:

1. *The goal is unclear.* Ill-structured problems do not lend themselves to setting clear and measurable goals, nor can they be easily solved by a single goal. Rather, ill-structured problems require setting and pursuing broader purposes and multiple goals.
2. *The means to achieve the goal is unclear.* When faced with an ill-structured problem, the specific goal that the leader will achieve has yet to be established, and there is no clear-cut procedure or way to achieve the goal. The problem the leader faces is novel, requiring the leader to, in turn, create a novel solution.
3. *Stakeholders and observers will disagree on success.* Solving an ill-structured problem results in a solution, but experts will not agree that the solution is the best one. In other words, solving ill-structured problems often leaves different groups with different interests unsatisfied because the nature of the problem is so complex that there will be little agreement as to when "success" has been achieved.

When leaders view their work from a more complex lens of analysis, they gain an advantage by understanding the limits (and possibilities) of their leadership and those of their followers. Of course, not all problems faced by leaders are ill structured. A significant part of learning-directed leadership practice, however, begins with ill-structured problem solving, not simple traditional management problems. One example of engaging in work in a more complex manner is found in the building of the Internet.

EXAMPLE: BUILDING THE INTERNET

In 1972, a group of graduate students thought about how to get geographically distributed sets of computers to talk to each other. The US government, through the Department of Defense, was funding a program to link a group of computers housed at a university across the country. The ultimate goal was to create a system for the universities to share research findings quickly and communicate with each other in an efficient manner.

The graduate students wanted to move the project along, but they encountered a significant problem. There was no common way for these computers to communicate. Although computers could share some limited amounts of data, there was not a standard communication format. It was like trying to open a door, but each person had a different size and shape of key. If the computer network was going to work, they needed a common key, which they called a protocol. The students became tired of waiting for someone to tell them what to do, so they developed a protocol themselves.

By 1977, well after most of the initial group of students had become fully employed research scientists, these university-based networks were beginning to communicate, and by 1983 a standard was established, and about 400 computers could now communicate on a regular basis. The result of this teamwork: the modern-day Internet. As this group of young engineers knew, leadership is much more about seeing things in new ways than it is about solving old problems. It was the engagement of higher-order learning that led to the development of new protocols, networks, and technology. Without seeing the limitation of experience and actively trying to learn, there would be no significant innovation. In this case the limitation of experience wasn't just an individual's experience but a limitation of a community's experience. New technologies, an organization's culture, and institutional support all contribute to unlocking innovation in organizations. But it is through learning when significant innovation occurs.

The early days of the Internet show how higher-order learning contributes to leadership success. Leaders, by definition, must construct their own world; they cannot be passive recipients of their environment. They change it, they mold it, and they persist in these efforts even in the face of difficulty. Said another way, leadership is a process of *world construction*, not simply responding to existing, given problems. No matter how intelligent the founders of the Internet might have been, without the capacity to actively construct a new world, there would be no Internet. To learn at the highest levels requires leaders to engage in purposeful effort to construct the world in a new and better form.

Just like the Quick Reaction Force in the opening of this chapter, leading innovation in technology also requires unstructured problem solving, not linear equations. Even though technological know-how played an important role in the development of the Internet, the design did not emerge from a linear equation, a line of computer code, or a communication network. The Internet emerged as a group of geographically distributed research scientists engaged in a trial-and-error process looking at the world in a new way, unencumbered by the limits of prior experience.

Far too often, though, leaders fail to recognize the character of problems as ill structured. Our own research has shown that the most popular strategy to deal with ill-structured problems lies in drawing on direct experience. We asked a group of business students, both undergraduate and MBA students, to solve an ill-structured problem. We then coded their responses and found that as much as 70–80 percent of the time, participants drew directly on their experience to solve the problem (Kayes, 2006a). While experience forms the basis of such decisions, only in about 20 percent of the cases did the participants go beyond their direct experience to recognize the problem as ill-structured; neither did they seek to solve the problem presented to them drawing on data other than experience. In only a few instances did the groups engage in independent critical thinking, challenge assumptions, demonstrate creativity in solving the problem, or display flexible reasoning. Importantly, this study relied primarily on the response of full- and part-time students. The part-time students were employed, many in formal management positions. It is not surprising that students who work primarily in the world of predefined problems presented by their professors (full-time students), would construct a problem in the simplest ways. What is surprising is the students who attend school part-time solve problems in a simple and incomplete way too. Fortunately, with experience, deliberate practice, and an appreciation of the higher-order learning, leaders can learn these skills.

Deliberate practice

A widely held myth of sorts has emerged in the world of leadership. Spread largely by Malcolm Gladwell's (2008) engaging prose, the myth goes something like this. To develop expertise, whether in chess, soccer, medicine, or business, take over 10,000 hours of practice. The implication is that to be in the top of any field takes many years. This "myth" is based largely on the pioneering work of psychologist Anders Ericsson (Ericsson and Lehmann, 1996). Ericsson does conclude, as Gladwell suggests, that 10,000 hours equates to expertise in many fields, but applying this rule to leadership requires reading beyond the headlines. From these 10,000 hours expertise does not magically appear. Expertise requires something Ericsson terms *deliberate practice*. Deliberate practice involves practice with a particular intensity that can only come from focused effort. In fact, Ericsson and his team conclude that deliberate practice requires such a high level of concentrated effort that a person can only engage in it for about 4 hours a day without facing burnout and fatigue. What this says is that practice in and of itself isn't enough. Expertise requires focus.

Recall Captain Self, the Quick Reaction Force leader introduced in the beginning of this chapter. Let's look at how he spent his time in the lead-up to Takur Ghar. How did he prepare for a battle he never knew he would fight? Accounts show that in Afghanistan, Self spent his days in a form of deliberate practice. After spending a full day training and briefing with his platoon of Rangers, Self retreated to the Command Center to observe enemy movements and US force response. During the time spent in the Command Center and in other forms of deliberate practice, such as studying prior combat situations and discussing army tactics and strategy with more experienced team members, Self learned. He then applied this learning to the battlefield. One result of engaging in deliberate practice is an unparalleled ability to predict the next move of an opponent. Self disagreed with repeated requests from his superiors to retreat down the mountain to alleged safety, only later to discover that enemy fighters were tactically positioned there.

Observation of experts and anticipation of competitor moves represent just a few aspects of deliberate practice revealed from Ericsson's research. The most important dimension of deliberate practice, we believe, is in its ties to learning. Deliberate practice involves "allowing continued improvement of performance in response to informative feedback" (p. 273). In other words, deliberate practice is distinguished from simple practice because learners engage in the task in such a way that continually challenges their current abilities. More than simply engaging in an activity for 10,000 hours, effective expertise requires learning in the form of observing, acting on feedback, and adjusting one's behaviors and beliefs based on new and evolving information.

A second problem with the "10,000-hour myth" lies in the kinds of problems faced by most leaders. Gladwell refers to the 10,000-hour rule in the context of "complex" problems. Yet, the expertise research has focused almost exclusively on well-structured problems—areas of performance where there are clear outcomes such as chess, sports activities, and even medical cases where a clear diagnosis can be reached. The research on expertise fails to reveal the role of deliberate practice on learning in the face of ill-structured problems. Simply because the structure of problems are different for leaders doesn't imply that the deliberate practice research doesn't apply. The notion of deliberate practice does hold promise in the study of leadership. In order to realize the role that deliberate practice plays in leadership development, we need to turn away from the simple structures of the laboratory, the chessboard, and the routine to the context of leadership.

A framework for the deliberate practice of leadership

Robert Kegan (1998), author of *In Over our Heads: The Mental Demands of Modern Life* and a noted developmental psychologist, offered an innovative framework for helping leaders to develop skills related to the deliberate practice of leadership. Kegan, along with other humanist psychologists, such as Abraham Maslow, believes in the potential of individuals to influence and guide their own learning. Kegan realizes that leaders don't have the luxury of taking their situation as a given. Rather, he suggests leaders *construct*, or actively participate in shaping their world. This is similar to what the team of research engineers did when building the Internet. Higher-order learning is not something that is given, but something that is achieved. It is through this construction process that leaders can continue to engage in deliberate practice even when they are at the top of their leadership game. For Kegan, higher-order learning is a process whereby leaders begin to better understand their relationship to others as well as the context in which those relationships exist. To navigate these demands, leaders must understand the contingencies, subjectivities, and uncertainties that lie at the core of leadership. After all, leadership is primarily an interpersonal activity, and learning to be a leader requires developing interpersonal skills.

Developing as a leader involves understanding, expressing, and taking action on inner contradictions that we hold as leaders. People find it difficult to uncover these hidden contradictions because revealing them might be uncomfortable. In order to feel and appear "rational" or non-contradictory in our beliefs, we choose not to recognize the contradiction. Ignoring the contradictions proves more workable, at least in the short term. However, in the long run, failing to recognize these inner contradictions holds us back.

Kegan and his colleague Lisa Lahey (2002) help leaders address these inner contradictions head on. The process helps leaders overcome natural pressures to hide these inner contradictions. To begin, leaders need a deeper understanding of the competing commitments they face. Competing commitments describe how two or more often conflicting and mutually exclusive goals coexist. By trying to preserve both goals, leaders end up achieving neither. Leaders can resolve these dilemmas by understanding the underlying assumptions that keep them from realizing a goal, resulting in a better understanding of how they, as leaders, construct their world. Importantly, when leaders recognize that they have a choice, they become more aware of their own learning and develop an understanding of what may be holding back their development.

Kegan and Lahey describe four "competing languages" that a leader must understand in order to develop higher-order learning. The first language contrasts complaint and commitment. Leaders are asked to complete the following sentence: "I am committed to the value or the importance of . . . ." With this question, the leader begins to express his or her values. The second language, the language of choice, contrasts blaming others with taking personal responsibility for commitments. How many times have we heard someone in an organization blame others for a situation without taking personal responsibility? With the second language, leaders ask, "What am I doing or not doing that prevents my commitment from being fully realized?"

The third language contrasts simply setting a short-term goal with realizing our full potential. Leaders are often tempted to achieve a short-term goal at the expense of long-term greatness. Identifying the third language helps leaders come to terms with this dilemma. Leaders are asked to explore the question: "What am I afraid of? What will I be seen as if my answer in language 2 is realized?" With this question leaders must confront their responsibility in relationship to language 2 that may be holding them back. Essentially, what rationalizations, explanations, or even excuses are people using to avoid taking responsibility for the situation? Instead of taking responsibility for a commitment, leaders may simply revert to blaming others to explain why it has not been achieved. Many leaders will find themselves stalled at language choice 3. Engaging in language 3 requires an honest struggle. The movement to level 3 points to a developmental shift, where leaders begin to see themselves as an active player in their own leadership. If they can actively engage in the third language, they begin to construct their own world. As leaders speak the third language, they expose their inner competing commitments. One action (or nonaction) pulls leaders toward their change; the other keeps them in the same place (p. 63).

If the third language were not challenging enough, the fourth language possesses even more difficulties. The fourth language marks the assumptions that hold us versus assumptions we hold. In this step, leaders uncover the underlying assumptions that drive thinking. If the third language increases awareness, the fourth language puts leaders in charge of writing their story. They are forced to ask: "What occurs or does not occur as a factor of these assumptions?" They may be forced to consider examples that contradict the assumptions. They will inevitably need to ask where the assumption comes from. Kegan and Lahey offer a step-by-step process to author one's own leadership. Using their techniques, leaders can come to terms with their own limitations and ways they can author their own leadership journey.

While the actual four-phase process requires more detail than we have provided, the reader can begin to see why this process is called uncovering your inner contradictions. The notion of competing commitments adds another layer on what it means for leaders to develop higher-order learning. First, as the research on deliberate practice suggests, developing leadership requires focusing intently on learning the skills, rules, and strategies of a domain over time. But for leaders, this kind of deliberate practice occurs only after leaders understand and succeed in ill-structured circumstances. Further, in order for deliberate practice to take shape, leaders must be able to take action in

Strategies for leaders

Some leadership consultants recommend resolving competing commitments by choosing sides. Others advocate imagining a paradox as being two ends of a pole where you should take the middle ground, finding a compromise between both positions. Others believe that you should transform a paradoxical problem into a logical, linear problem rather than resolving or removing it. We advocate an alternative approach based on Fredberg's study of CEOs. He and his colleagues found that when faced with many of the toughest decisions, leaders should learn how to focus on both sides of a situation at the same time and then clarify priorities and how these priorities influence actions. In summary:

▶ Recognize that your competing commitments are part of leading at any level.
▶ Make things happen simultaneously; avoid the "either/or" trap.
▶ Use action plans to focus on reprioritizing what is important in your life.

the face of competing commitments. The point is that situational awareness comes before or in conjunction with deliberate practice. Deliberate practice for leaders emerges from what those in the military call situational awareness (see Fletcher, 2004), the ability to respond to the unexpected. What we are suggesting is that situational awareness requires recognition of the situation and a comprehension of its dynamic nature in order for deliberate practice to emerge. To fully engage in deliberate practice, leaders first must understand the ill-structured nature and novelty of the problems they face, as well as a basic understanding of their own internal competing commitments and be willing to take action in the face of this knowledge. Leaders who develop these leadership skills will find it easier to try meta-learning. In the next section we return to the ultimate outcome of higher-order thinking: multiple forms of learning, challenging of mental models, and meta-learning.

The goals of higher-order learning

Meta-learning consists of two critical capacities. First is the capacity to engage in multiple forms of learning simultaneously, as demonstrated by

Captain Nate Self in the opening of this chapter. A second capacity is to engage in reshaping existing mental models. Mental models govern internal motivation and in turn behavior. Mental models are difficult to change because we are often unaware of them. Where competing commitments hold us back due to our own insecurities or assumptions about ourselves, mental models hold us back because of the assumptions we make about the outside world, including our prejudices and our assumptions about how the world works. Here is one way to think about mental models and how they can limit us as leaders. Let's assume, as any psychologist does, that we are all authors of our own leadership story. Said another way, each leader has a "narrative" that guides their behavior. If we are all authors of our own leadership narratives, what hidden assumptions lie deep within those narratives?

Boje (2001) offers some strategies for unearthing these hidden models based on the notion of deconstruction of narratives. To uncover these hidden assumptions, Boje urges us to start by thinking of a situation. In this case, we will use the example of a friend, a salesperson, who was considering applying for an internal promotion to manager. What would it mean to be in charge of her former peers, an outspoken and disgruntled bunch of salesman? She suspected that these sales professionals might try to undermine her authority. To overcome her fear and uncover her hidden mental models she engaged in the following eight-step process.

1. *Duality search*. She made a list of any one-sided terms. An example is a where she wrote down the words "undermine," "sabotage," and "disgruntled." She realized through this simple step that her cognitive model was that her peers were completely "bad" and she was viewing the situation through a very narrow and oppressive lens.
2. *Reinterpreting the hierarchy*. Dissect any hierarchical relationships present in a narrative and reinterpret the hierarchy. An example is where, she thought, as a manager she would dominate the actions of her subordinates; she changed this and thought about how after her promotion they would be a team, with shared power.
3. *Rebel voices*. With this step, you think about what others would say if they disagreed with you. This can be an imagined "other" or a real "other." Here, the "would-be manager," imagined what her grandmother would say about the situation. Her grandmother had passed away many years prior, but had been a strong and forceful presence in her life. The grandmother as a "rebel voice" told her what a great opportunity it would be for her and that she could change the dynamic on her team with some skill and patience.

4. *Other side of the story.* Find the other sides of the story, as stories always have multiple sides. You reverse the story so that what is emphasized initially becomes marginal, what is vertical becomes horizontal, and so on. The aspiring manager changed her perception of the situation where the reporting relationships and the people dynamic were minimal and redesigning the product line and executing a brilliant sales strategy were central.

5. *Denying the plot.* Unearth the type of plot imagined and change it to another type of plot. In this case, her narrative of becoming a manager sounded more like a "tragedy," and we encouraged her to think of it as a "comedy."

6. *Finding the exception.* Every difficult situation is subject to rules and scripts that can be identified and changed. An example is where you change a seemingly logical conclusion about an outcome and reconsider a seemingly absurd outcome as an alternative. In this case, her conclusion that her peers would be disgruntled at her promotion and might try to sabotage her effectiveness was changed to her peers being delighted at her leadership and becoming unified around their desire for positive change.

7. *Tracing what is between the lines.* You fill in the blanks and add more script to the backstage or the in-between. An example is where she adds history or context to the story she has written. She recalled her history of being hired as a sales assistant, early in her career, while others from her graduating class were not hired. She experienced their scorn and envy, and it stuck with her many years later.

8. *Resituate.* The final step is where you completely reconfigure the initial narrative that was imagined. The final interpretation of the situation is completely different from the initial interpretation (Kayes, A. 2007).

CHALLENGING AND REFORMULATING MENTAL MODELS

Douglas McGregor (1960) put forth an idea on mental models that has stood the test of time. He believed that leaders held different views on the "nature of an employee in an organization." These deeply held beliefs or mental models caused many leaders to mismanage situations. McGregor theorized that managers view employees through one of two mental models: Theory X leaders believe that people are basically lazy and need incentives to learn; Theory Y leaders believe that people are basically self-actualized and enjoy learning. These beliefs stem from a leader's mental models about how and why people learn. Not only do our mental models

Table 4 **The nature of employees in an organization**

Theory X mental model	Theory Y mental model
Employees dislike work.	Employees naturally enjoy work.
Employees must be motivated or coerced into working.	Employees are self-directed and will motivate themselves.
The average person must be given responsibility.	The average person will seek out responsibility.
Employees will avoid work without strict rules and enforced policies,	Employees will strive to do their best even without close supervision.

Strategies for leaders

Take some time to look at the descriptors in Table 4.

▶ Which set of beliefs hold true for the way that you view employees? Once you've decided which is your mental model, you can then begin to challenge and reformulate it.

▶ When did someone surprise you and not fit into your beliefs? For example, if you identified with the Theory X approach to viewing employees, when did someone not fit your mental model and request additional work and take initiative far beyond her role?

▶ Take time out of your day to notice these inconsistencies and build your new insights into your work practices.

▶ Practice management techniques for both types of employees.

hold us back as leaders, they also hold back others being led. McGregor shows us how a leader's mental model can prevent others from learning too. In order to facilitate learning in others, leaders need to challenge their own assumptions about the nature of their followers and how these assumptions hold back everyone's learning.

Barriers to higher-order learning: Robert E. Lee during the Civil War

To highlight the importance of higher-order learning and caution about the barriers to learning, we conclude with another military story, that of General Robert E. Lee in the US Civil War. Historians continue to hold heated debates about the leadership of General Robert E. Lee, a key general leading the army of Northern Virginia during the US Civil War. Lee's opponents in the Union/Northern States Army held a significant advantage over the South, where Lee stood command. Despite being consistently outmatched in size and resources, Lee's army emerged as victorious in the early days of the Civil War. Lee seemed to possess something his rivals, Union generals like McClellan and Burnside, did not. Lee possessed an unparalleled ability to learn.

We know of Lee's impressive ability to learn from his writing. He kept meticulous journals and issued written orders throughout his life. He began writing as early as 1840, into the Mexican War, and continued writing throughout the Civil War. He wrote about his first victorious battle in September of 1862, his humiliating loss against General Meade at Gettysburg in July 1863, and his eventual concession to General Grant in April of 1865. His journals continued after the war. From these journals, an interesting picture of Lee's higher-order learning, and its eventual deterioration, begins to emerge.

A group of psychologists wanted to understand Lee's learning; so they conducted a detailed review of his writings (Suedfeld, Corteen, and McCormick, 1986). They looked closely for something called integrative complexity, a way of thinking that tracks closely with higher-order learning. Both the concept of integrative complexity and higher-order learning describe how well a leader identifies and processes new opportunities.

Specifically, leaders deemed high on the scale of higher-order learning are flexible learners, oriented toward seeking out new and challenging ideas. They consider multiple viewpoints. At the low end of the higher-order learning scale are those who demonstrate rigid thinking. They take an all-or-nothing approach rather than looking at options and various details. Sometimes those on the lower end of the higher-order learning scale may see only their own individual interests and make decisions that, in the long run, prove to be counterproductive for the larger organization. The researchers used a ranking system, with 1 indicating low levels and 5 indicating high levels of higher-order learning.

The study revealed something remarkable about Lee's higher-order learning. At the onset of war, Lee showed the signs of higher-order learning at the high end of the scale. In fact, researchers regularly scored his insights at 5 out of 5 possible points. He reached some of his highest scores at the start of the war. At the same time, he ranked significantly higher than his Union opponents, who ranked only 2 or sometimes 3. Over the course of the war, dramatic changes occurred in Lee's ability to learn. Lee's higher-order learning declined as the war continued and reached its lowest level around May of 1864. This was the time of his second decisive loss to General Grant at the battle of Spotsylvania. For the first time in the war, Lee's higher-order learning even dipped below that of his opponent, General Grant. As the war drew to its conclusion and Lee's army continued its losses, his higher-order learning even dipped below that of his opposing generals. In the same analysis, the researchers noticed that the higher-order learning of the Union generals never increased significantly but stayed steady throughout the war. By the war's final battles, however, the opposing Northern generals demonstrated a slight advantage in higher-order learning. Finally, Lee regained his earlier levels of higher-order learning in his few short years after the war.

Historians could have a field day debating these findings. Some argue that Lee's decreasing ability to learn resulted from heart trouble and related factors that ailed Lee during the war. Others argue that Lee stopped keeping his journals after his written orders fell into enemy hands. Lee stopped keeping detailed written notes after his victory at Antietam, making it difficult to track his learning at all. Both historical explanations, however, miss at least two important points on learning.

Lee's declining health only supports the notion that higher-order learning fluctuates by exposing some of the ways that a leader's learning can become vulnerable. Studies on the physiology of learning are beginning to reveal some interesting relationships between physical health and our ability to learn. For example, studies are beginning to show that physical health correlates with mental health and that learning can be tracked to sleeping patterns and quantity of sleep. Further, many studies are beginning to reveal that, although some decline in learning ability is inevitable over time, some of the age-related declines in our ability to learn can be forestalled and even reversed with physical fitness and training. Carol Hoare (2006), one of our colleagues at The George Washington University Graduate School of Education and Human Development, has compiled a thoughtful look at the relationship between learning and development that summarizes these findings. Lee's physical health was declining over the course of the war only further confirms the evidence that Lee's higher-order learning also decreased.

Lee's declining health may have contributed to his decline in learning, but something even more telling may have been trampling Lee's ability to learn at the highest levels: stress. The increased time pressure to make decisions, continual loss of resources, danger, and constant fatigue each must have played a role. Supervisors and subordinates demands unwittingly assured that Lee faced a constant overload of information as well. As the war dragged on, facing stress and information overload, Lee's higher-order learning continued to deteriorate. Even prior experience may have had a negative impact. Despite its benefits, experience itself may have actually had a negative impact on learning. Lee's confidence grew as his army expelled Northern forces from the South. Even when Lee's armies faced opponents with significantly more soldiers, Lee's army proved dominant. It seemed that Lee became more and more confident in his army's ability to dominate in battle, even when the odds were against him. It is the notion that Lee, emboldened by his surprising early victories over his opponents, relied too much on his past experiences and not enough on learning and innovation. According to some historians, Lee may have become overconfident and began to take unreasonable risks. As Lee gained confidence, he may have also become increasingly unable to learn. The negative effects of experience began to set in. His ability to innovate may have decreased as well. As his tactics in victory became embedded in his mind, he became less adaptable to new and innovative methods. His early successes may have also trapped the general in overconfidence and led him to underestimate his opponent. Figure 13 maps this decline and regeneration over time.

The study doesn't decisively prove that the ability to learn was directly related to Lee's losing the Civil War. War, like other leadership activity, is too complex to explain through a limited number of variables. Still, the steady decline in Lee's integrative complexity highlights several important lessons. The circumstances surrounding General Lee provide

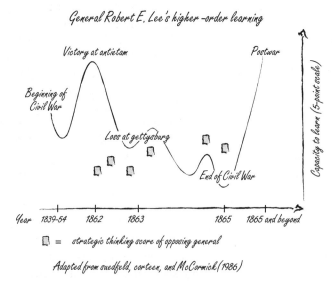

Figure 13 **Challenges to General Robert E. Lee's ability to learn**

a potent reminder that higher-order learning requires constant attention. Whatever the type of organization, environmental challenges will provide a constant threat to higher-order learning. Building higher-order learning requires effort, and maintaining it requires constant effort too. As leaders navigate the stressful and complex world of organizations, learning provides an advantage.

Conclusion

When leaders engage in higher-order learning, they move beyond commonplace explanations and seek new and innovative approaches. Higher-order learning requires looking at situations from a new viewpoint, challenging conventional wisdom, and accepting contradictory information with an open mind. We can break down higher-order learning into the following parts, experience, deliberate practice and meta-learning. First, leaders hold only a value-laden perspective, often a single immovable viewpoint. This viewpoint often emerges from direct experience or simple opinion and includes broad generalizations and often stereotyping. But in order to achieve higher-order learning, leaders begin to recognize different viewpoints and utilize multiple information sources. Deliberate practice facilitates leadership development through growth. Leaders make connections between seemingly divergent viewpoints. They can see distinctions between different variables and how interactions between variables can affect one another. Finally, leaders try multiple and overlapping types of learning. Learning leaders recognize that "today's solutions lead to tomorrow's problems," thus recognizing potential unintended consequences.

Questions for reflection

1. What are some of the ill-structured problems that I face?
2. What types of learning have produced my best learning experiences? What types of learning have produced my worst learning experiences?
3. How can I improve on my ability to recognize and respond to different viewpoints?
4. How can I better anticipate and manage unintended consequences?

5 Building Resilience

Key ideas

▶ Resilience involves learning in the face of adversity, stress, or crisis.
▶ Leaders learn to persevere in the face of cognitive, physiological, and environmental challenges.
▶ Leaders foster efficacy, the belief that one is capable of success, by supporting learning and development through coaching and mentoring.
▶ Leaders balance measured optimism with depressive realism.
▶ Leaders build resilient organizations by planning for failure, fostering innovation, facilitating social networks based on positive thought and action, demonstrating a time orientation based on achievement over time, and valuing the development of self and others.

In this chapter we explore how leaders learn to deal with difficult situations, work through their fears or hesitations, and respond to failure. Leading can often be challenging; however, with knowledge, confidence, and a desire to learn, leaders can overcome many challenges. We learn from frontline army officers, from a lab experiment designed to help a patient with a crippling fear of snakes, as well as from other situations. Leaders build resilience in themselves and in others through learning, and specific factors enhance or prevent this learning. Resilience describes *the ability to adapt in the face of adversity, stress, crisis, and error. It involves recovering from challenging experiences and setbacks.* Resilience involves adaptation and recovering from failure (e.g., American Psychological Association, n.d.). We begin by looking at Steve Jobs of Apple Computer and what has been called one of the best graduation speeches of the decade.

A leader's story: Steve Job's failure and resilience

In the 1970s a new hobby began to emerge in garages across the United States. Mostly young men, intelligent but perhaps socially challenged, spent hours and hours creating electronic devices about the size of a breadbox. The first personal computers were just that, a device made by individuals for their personal use (Wu, 2010). It took a man by the name of Steve Jobs, possessing a broader vision of the potential of these little boxes, to transform this obscure hobby into a business. Jobs, the cofounder of Apple along with Steve Wozniak, built one of the world's most respected companies.

Starting a company proved less challenging than keeping it running. The board of directors fired Steve Jobs in the late 1980s from the company he founded. Later, he reflected that this "failure" provided the best source of material from which to learn. He remarked on the importance of resilience in a commencement speech to Stanford University students in 2005. By the time Jobs had reached the ripe age of 30, he had built a US $2 billion business with 4,000 employees. "Then I got fired," explained Jobs. "What had been the focus of my entire adult life was gone, and it was devastating. I really didn't know what to do for a few months." Jobs considered retiring from the job he loved altogether. "I was still in love" with the business of technology and being an entrepreneur he soon realized. After a period of reflection, Jobs entered what he called "one of the most creative periods of my life." Time off from the day-to-day work of running a company created time to reflect, fall in love, get married, and start a family.

One of the most influential creations to emerge from Jobs' "time off" from Apple may have been the development of Pixar, the first company to develop a computer-animated full-length cartoon. In another twist, during his break from running a major company, Jobs established a new computer company called NeXT, which would eventually be purchased by his old company, Apple. The turn of events returned Jobs to the head position at Apple. "I'm pretty sure none of this would have happened if I hadn't been fired from Apple. It was awful-tasting medicine, but I guess the patient needed it."

Jobs described resilience in a professional situation, but resilience isn't limited to career decisions. Many facets of life require resilience. Some might argue that Jobs is unique and in many ways he is; however, many leaders learn the kind of resilience described by Jobs. For some, resilience may well prove second nature, but a string of research studies leading back nearly a quarter century suggests otherwise. People learn resilience, albeit in many cases slowly.

The need for resilience

Never before has resilience been so critical to the success of leaders. Take the economic crisis as an example of the environmental hardships that leaders face. In late 2008 and early 2009, the constriction of worldwide economic growth was evidenced in the United States by an unemployment rate that hovered around 10 percent. The US Bureau of Labor Statistics reported that over 4.4 million jobs were lost in 2007 alone. Those who remained employed faced dramatic budget cuts, the prospect of future job losses, and reorganizations. Change had been a buzzword in leadership for decades, but never before had leaders been tested in their ability to lead through this type of change. The crisis only heightened the frenetic, stressful, and fast-paced workplace. It is not overstating the case to say that not in a generation has building resilience in oneself and others been more critical.

Figure 14 shows the factors that affect resilience. Given the critical need for leaders to adapt and recover from setbacks, it is encouraging that resilience can be learned, just as any set of skills can be learned (Coutu, 2002b). We are not born with a predetermined measure of resilience like we are with other characteristics such as height and hair color.

Learning resilience through experience

Resilience involves a set of skills, abilities, and behaviors that leaders can learn over time and through experience. Learning to be resilient begins

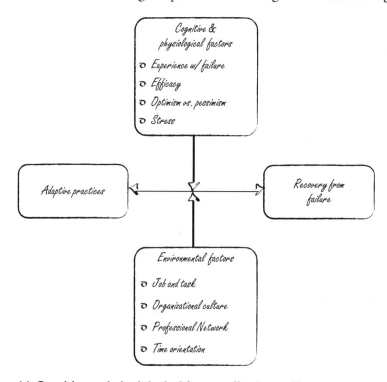

Figure 14 **Cognitive and physiological factors affecting resilience**

in childhood, according to a study published by The Young Foundation. The aptly titled *The State of Happiness Report* detailed the results of the first year of a 3-year project teaching resilience to 2,000 children aged 11–13 in schools in the United Kingdom (Shandro et al., 2010). The study found that children are naturally adaptive and can learn new patterns of behavior. Specifically, children develop motivation to learn and improve resilience. The study listed several factors that contribute to the early development of resilience: (1) being given different cognitive tools to explain individual circumstances; (2) being rewarded for showing effort rather than for innate intellectual ability; and (3) being encouraged to believe that you can and will make a difference in your communities. Researchers tried to change existing beliefs about failure by encouraging *attempts* at change rather than trying to achieve actual results.

The study revealed four ways to boost resilience. First, experience at failure played a role in building resilience. Repeated failures tended to lower resilience, but even small successes raised resilience. Second, modeling teaches resilience. Modeling, or comparing oneself to someone with similar capabilities with mastery of a task, improves resilience as individuals build confidence in the task and learn strategies for success. Third, resilience is a social process. Observing someone else bounce back from failure or achieve or succeed builds confidence. This is why people can learn effectively from a mentor. Fourth, social persuasion through positive verbal encouragement helps to build resilience, while criticism lowers it. When told that they are a failure, individuals' confidence diminishes. Fifth, physiological factors—physical signs of stress and distress—lower resilience as well (Shandro et al., 2010).

Just like the children in the study, the resilient leader remains open to new ways of thinking, shows a willingness to bounce back from adversity or failure, and develops an evolving set of skills that adapt to changing situations. Specifically, resilient leaders continually develop new and varied competencies and improve their ability to assess and make decisions in a situation, all the while remaining humble and inclusive (Reid, 2008).

Research that supports the positive effects of resilience goes beyond children. Researchers at the Center for Creative Leadership found a similar effect in leaders who experience challenging situations. Leaders who had experienced setbacks found themselves better positioned in the long term and experienced more career growth and success than those who had only successes (Martin, 2010). Challenging situations caused leaders to learn by trying out new ideas, testing new behaviors, learning new skills, and reflecting on their leadership skills. The researchers described how early successes actually drove failure in some leaders. For example, they found that leaders who experienced a string of successes early in their career might actually be less likely to experience long-term growth. Failure, it seems, proved critical for leaders to develop, grow, and prosper in the long term.

The role of self-efficacy in learning

Psychologist Albert Bandura spent a lifetime studying something he called self-efficacy. His research spawned numerous studies on the connection between efficacy, learning, and mastery. Bandura (1997) found that efficacy emerges when focusing on small gains in mastery toward a larger goal. This resulting positive experience magnifies the confidence of individuals over time and increases their capacity to try again, even after failure. Self-efficacy describes how a leader judges his or her capabilities in performing a job or task. Most psychologists believe that efficacy is not something a leader is born with, but something that emerges from experience with success. As leaders learn and gain confidence in their abilities, they develop a sense of security, confidence, and optimism that they can exercise a degree of control over success.

"MARY'S" EFFORTS TO OVERCOME HER FEAR OF SNAKES

"Mary," a composite character developed from all the participants in one study led by Albert Bandura, illustrates the generative power of building self-efficacy—that is, the confidence one feels having successfully performed a set of actions. Mary was afraid of snakes, a condition called ophidiophobia. This was no run-of-the-mill, garden-variety fear, but one physician would describe as a clinical phobia. Her phobia was so bad that after reading that a snake had gotten loose in the sewer system of a neighboring town, Mary could not use her bathroom for fear that the snake might be lurking in her toilet. She had also given up outdoor activities because of the fear of being harassed by snakes. This made Mary's plight even more debilitating, for, as a geologist, her livelihood depended on going into the wild. Yet she could hardly enter her own backyard, let alone grasslands full of snakes.

To better understand Mary's plight, researchers enrolled her in a study along with 35 other people who also had severe snake phobia. First, the research team tested the seriousness of Mary's phobia. Mary began, nervously, by observing from behind a glass panel a 3-foot boa constrictor sitting safely inside a glass tank. Once Mary had managed the simple observation through glass, the researcher removed the barrier. Now Mary was looking directly down at the snake from above. Even though the snake could not reach Mary, she trembled as she watched. Over several sessions, Mary built up a reasonable level of comfort with the snake. She could sit in the same room while the snake sat safely in the glass tank.

Next, the researchers suggested that she touch the snake with a glove. This, too, proved challenging at first, but over time, Mary learned to reach into the tank and touch the constrictor. She was making significant progress. The next step was to hold the snake with her ungloved hands. Over time, Mary achieved this feat too before moving on to the next step, which involved moving the snake closer to her face. After several sessions, Mary proved ready for the final step: sitting in a chair with her hands held down by her side as the snake freely climbed across her lap. Although Mary could grab the snake and throw it off, or even dart up from the chair and run away, she did not. It appeared that she had overcome her phobia. In her final exercise, Mary retrieved the snake as it freely slithered around the room and returned it to its cage. At the end of each session, Mary rated her level of anxiety from 1 to 10. In the first session, Mary could hardly bear to look the snake in the eyes through a protective sheet of glass, and the session ended after only a few moments. The psychologists running the study assigned her a counselor. The counselor proceeded to work through each step first so Mary could observe as the counselor engaged the snake. The counselor also offered her an aid to help her in each new step, for example, by guiding Mary through each step and even

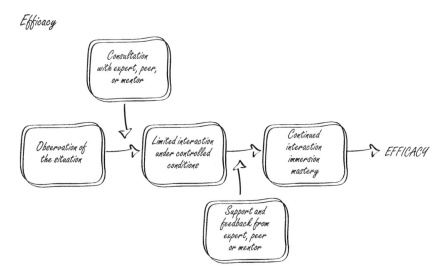

Figure 15 **Building efficacy**

joining her on occasion, giving her extra-heavy gloves, or removing the large snake and replacing it with a smaller, less intimidating one. Figure 15 shows this process.

ELEMENTS OF SELF-EFFICACY: MODELING, CONFIDENCE, AND MOTIVATION

When she began, Mary could tolerate only a few brief moments with the snake, but by the end of her treatment her encounters lasted nearly 45 minutes. Eventually, Mary had almost completely overcome her fear of snakes. The psychologists who conducted the study noted the importance of the subject working with a counselor or watching the counselor work through each step. Psychologists have come to call this process *modeling*. This involves a person observing another more competent person perform a task, learning from it, and then trying to perform the task himself or herself. At the time these studies were conducted, modeling had already been established as an important process of learning, so the experimenters didn't in fact take too much notice of it. However, the psychologists found another attribute of equal or greater importance than modeling.

Mary and others who were successful in overcoming their phobias relied on a counselor to help them in some of the most difficult moments; however, the most successful learners did not rely exclusively on the counselor. It seemed that Mary was building a sense of self-confidence in her own ability to deal with fear and anxiety, which were holding her back from being able to handle the situation. Her fear of failure and the related anxiety were actually lowering her own ability to learn and change. But as Mary's confidence grew, so did her ability to perform. It seemed that confidence to complete the task also led to an improvement in her ability to perform the task.

Mary learned how to build confidence in herself, overcome fear of failure, and learn methods to take control of specific elements of her environment. She developed self-efficacy. Self-efficacy is different from self-esteem, in that self-esteem has to do with individuals' sense of self-worth, while self-efficacy has to do with their sense of their abilities in a given situation. For example, Mary could have easily had high self-esteem, even though she had low efficacy at the start of her therapy regarding her handling of snakes. At the same time, simply because she improved her mastery in working with snakes doesn't imply she held herself in any greater esteem.

Efficacy is an important part of resilience because low self-efficacy in leaders is often translated into feelings of hopelessness, and hopelessness can result in the inability to act out of fear of failure or anxiety. In addition, those with low efficacy often distort perceptions, making a task appear harder or more dangerous than it is. On the other hand, leaders with high self-efficacy and the ability to build efficacy in others will find that they can persist at a task, even if there are failures or setbacks. Leaders who build efficacy in others believe that they are in control of their own lives, take stock of failure, and attempt to reconsider circumstances in order to gain a greater sense of control over them. Even more important for learning, leaders with high efficacy are more likely to learn or try a new task. Efficacy and motivation are connected; high efficacy likely leads to an intensity of effort and persistence. Mary's ability to overcome her fears illustrates how self-efficacy leads to overcoming challenges. Working with a trained professional, Mary was able to understand, even control her emotions and eventually overcome her fears. As she gained a sense of control over her immediate circumstances, she learned that many of the limitations she faced were in her mind.

THE LIMITS OF SELF-EFFICACY: FEELING LIKE YOU HAVE CONTROL—EVEN WHEN YOU DON'T

If building self-efficacy worked this way in every situation, many individuals could overcome their fears simply by enrolling in a study like the one Mary completed. Despite the impressive results of Mary and many of those like her, consider also that there are limits to efficacy. Resilience doesn't mean blind faith in one's own abilities, nor does it signal that a person has the skills to deal with every situation. Even Albert Bandura recognized that efficacy has limits, especially in the face of risky or unpredictable tasks. Mary's progress, despite the promising nature of its outcome, should be observed with some reservations as well. Not all situations can be overcome simply through the power of the mind. In fact, the mind can be easily tricked into believing it exercises more control over its environment than it actually does. A series of experiments reminds us how easy it is to trick ourselves into believing we exercise control over our outcomes, even when we don't.

Psychologist Daniel Wegner (1989) may be best known for his study of white bears—not real white bears, but imaginary ones. He asked subjects in a controlled study not to think about white bears. The harder the subjects tried not to think about white bears, the more the thought of white bears appeared in their mind. The harder they tried to control their thoughts, the less they could. From these initial studies, Wegner began to unravel the limits of control over our own minds. After decades of study, Wegner concluded that people actually have less control over their mental activity than they think. His recent research reveals the power of self-deception.

A research team led by Wegner conducted an experiment to see if they could manipulate an individual's feelings of self-control. They asked whether someone could mistake the action of another and think it was his own. To find out, Wegner placed an experimental subject in front of a mirror. A curtain hung directly behind each subject and the curtain had holes cut in the location of the individual's arms. Behind the curtain a second person placed her arms through the holes and extended her arms in front of the subject. The subject, therefore, could see the arms of the second person, but not the rest of their body. In fact, by looking in the mirror, the subject might even believe that the arms of the individual behind the curtain belonged to him. Next, Wenger and his team instructed the individual behind the curtain to move her arms in various ways. Both the person behind the curtain and the subject could hear the instructions. The researchers varied the timing of the instructions too. With one group, they would introduce the instructions before the action; in other cases they would introduce the instructions and the person behind the curtain would move simultaneously. An outside observer too might believe the arms belonged to the subject in front of the curtain. But in reality, it was the person behind the curtain whose arms were moving.

The seemingly complicated experiment resulted in a simple finding. The experiment revealed a lot about a person's efficacy—how much a person feels they can control themselves and their environment. Even though the subjects had no direct control over the arms they saw in the mirror, they could be tricked into believing they were responsible for moving the arms behind them. When the researcher instructed the person behind the curtain to move her arms, the subject in front of the curtain reported higher confidence that he had actually done the moving! In other words, despite the fact that the subject had no control over the arms of the other person, simply hearing the commands increased his feelings of control over the situation. In particular, those who heard the instructions before or at the same time as the actual movement by the other person were more likely to report they had control over the other person's arms, even though they did not directly control the movement.

Wegner concluded that individuals can be made to believe that they have control of an action, even when they do not. If individuals know an action is about to occur, or that action occurs simultaneously with an instruction, they become "primed" to believe that they have more control over the movement than they actually possess. The study brings up important questions about leadership. For example, under what circumstances is a leader likely to miscalculate his or her level of control over a situation?

Taken together, the studies on efficacy and self-control suggest areas where individuals can learn mastery in particular situations, but show the limits of increased feelings of efficacy due to overestimation of the control. We can draw a few preliminary conclusions about resilience. First, like the findings of the UK school children, resilience is a social process in the sense that others often prime our beliefs about our own potential. In both the efficacy studies as well as the studies on self-control, social influence is paramount to change. The role of a leader, mentor, and coach in building resilience cannot be overstated. Second, it becomes easy to confuse our own actions, and their ultimate causes, with the actions of others, especially when we share the same goal. We might take this a step further and suggest that one way leaders can improve their resilience is to build shared goals with team members. These shared feelings of achievement can build team members' beliefs around their potential. That is, a sense of accomplishment in a group is based on shared experiences of achievement, and these shared experiences in turn will boost future confidence around the ability to achieve more difficult goals. The third implication of these studies is that resilience may be related to expectations. Recall that individuals reported higher levels of control when they were given instructions about the action prior to the actual action. In terms of building resilience, changing expectations and boosting people's sense of control are important elements of dealing with change. It is also helpful to understand how people evaluate a situation not just based on confidence and control, but also on how positive or negative they perceive it to be.

Optimism, pessimism, and learning

In Chapter 4 we described the importance of higher-order learning for leaders. As leaders engage in higher-order learning, they begin to see situations in a more complete way, learn mechanisms to deal with complexity, and learn to act in the face of competing demands. A connection between higher-order learning and resilience comes in considering pessimism. Studies on optimism often characterize individuals into two sorts. Pessimistic individuals see the world as stable, attribute problems or setbacks to global factors that are beyond their control, and focus on their limitations as an individual. In contrast, optimistic individuals see the world as changeable. There is nothing that can't be changed (see, for example, Peterson, Waldman, Balthazard, and Thatcher, 2008). Optimists believe that most situations can be controlled either through hard work or improvement. They also tend to believe that hardship is limited, circumstantial, and often short lived (see, for example, Satterfield, 2000, pp. 349–51). It would be easy to make the leap and say that optimists tend to be better learners and therefore, more resilient.

An even bolder judgment would be to suggest that optimists are better leaders. But this is not the case.

To understand why optimism itself is not an indicator of learning or leadership, it helps to return to research and an idea called *depressive realism*. An emerging body of research on depressive realism suggests that those with symptoms of depression are more pessimistic in their outlook. This makes sense in that we would expect depressed individuals to look at the world more pessimistically. But depressive realism went a step further. It pointed to research that said depressed individuals were actually more accurate in their predictions of future events. In particular, depressive individuals were more accurate than optimists in predicting the occurrence of negative events. Thus, the notion of depressive realism suggested that depression led to greater accuracy in predicting future events because depressive individuals were better at identifying potential roadblocks or negative occurrences. The idea is that optimists tend to be biased because they look at a situation and become overconfident, missing potential roadblocks. In contrast, the pessimist tends to look at a situation and see the potential for negative results. The question became which was better: to "see the world through rose-colored glasses" like the optimist or to be "sadder but wiser" like the pessimist.

Over the years, studies on the relationship between optimism, pessimism, and accuracy have reported mixed findings (Dobson and Franche, 1989; Strunk, Lopez, and DeRubeis, 2006; Ackermann and DeRubeis, 1991; Wunderley, Reddy, and Dember, 1998). In some cases, optimists appear to be more accurate at predicting events; in other cases, pessimists appear to be more accurate. The important point for learning-directed leadership is that optimism and pessimism in individuals may be related to learning. This has caused some resilience experts to suggest that optimism and pessimism are of relative value to higher-order learning. Figure 16 graphically illustrates a relationship between these factors that was suggested by Satterfield (2000, p. 354). The model distinguishes between measured optimism and reckless optimism and between depressive realism and helpless depressiveness. In contrast to the measured optimist, who considers limitations, the reckless optimist fails to take into account context and potential challenges or is unable to make a realistic assessment of a situation. The helpless depressive is likely to consider only the negative aspects, looking for criticism without considering potential benefits. In contrast, the depressive realist may identify limitations and challenges and bring up blind spots, but may

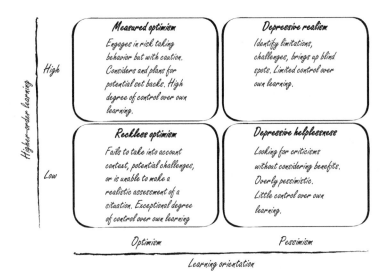

Figure 16 **Optimism, pessimism, and higher-order learning**

not look at the down side of a situation. Leaders need to consider that neither pessimism nor optimism in and of itself supports resilience. Understanding how leaders and their followers assess a situation can help with resilience.

Factors in resilience

Efficacy, control, and level of optimism are cognitive aspects of resilience. These factors determine how we gather, process, and take action on information. Physiological and environmental factors also play a role in learning to be resilient.

PHYSIOLOGICAL FACTORS: STRESS

Have you ever noticed two people in the same workplace, with one exhibiting a high level of stress and the other person, in a similar situation, experiencing little stress? The difference may be in how an individual interprets stress. The first person likely experiences stress as a hindrance, whereas the second person likely experiences stress as a challenge. Leadership involves understanding the difference between these two types of stress (LePine, LePine, and Jackson, 2004). Challenge stressors, such as a heavy workload or pressure to complete tasks in a specific amount of time, enhance the achievement of goals. People often report feeling exhilarated under stressful conditions while achieving their goals, but this exhilaration is usually due to challenge stressors, not hindrance stressors. Hindrance stressors prevent people from achieving their goals. Confusion over responsibilities, inadequate resources, or office politics usually leads to hindrance stress. Hindrance stress in particular can lead to physiological challenges including headaches, high blood pressure, heart disease, anxiety, and depression. From an organizational standpoint, these can ultimately lead to absenteeism, loss of job satisfaction, and diminished productivity.

ENVIRONMENTAL FACTORS: EXTENT OF JOB STRUCTURE AND FLEXIBILITY

Stress and other physiological factors lower resilience, the ability to adapt and recover, in some leaders. Other leaders may be constrained in building resilience simply because of the nature of their job. Despite these constraints it is possible to learn resilience, but the learning process depends on the leader. For instance, some jobs are highly structured; they leave little room for individuals to exercise judgment in how the specific tasks of the job are performed. But there is always some latitude for leaders, even in highly structured conditions. Consider for instance the captain of a fire station, whose job is highly unstructured. Each emergency situation is different, and firefighters are trained to exercise judgment and analyze all the different aspects of the fire such as elapsed time, type of fire, and the impact and safety of themselves and potential occupants and onlookers. Even nonemergency situations are unstructured. A firefighter may be dispatched to build relationships in the community by staffing a parade or a marathon or to assist in city elections. This type of job structure promotes adaptation as the captain responds rapidly to different situations.

An example of someone with a structured job is Helen, a warehouse manager that we worked with in a food services manufacturing organization. There are specific rules and procedures around inventory levels and inbound and outbound shipments in this company. Each transaction is based on a predefined schedule. Although there are more situational constraints for leaders in highly structured jobs, they can still integrate creativity and problem solving into their job. Helen chose not to be constrained by her job, building adaptive processes into the workflow that redefined the inventory tracking system in her warehouse. She implemented a barcode system that made inventory tracking more efficient, and she provided forklift certification classes for all her staff. They moved from being specialists, which slowed down the inventory process when a forklift driver wasn't on hand, to being expert generalists. Any of Helen's employees could step in and manage the inventory process from arrival to delivery.

Resilient leaders continually challenge themselves by viewing their job as fluid, leaving plenty of room for exercising judgment. When we compare the job of firefighter with that of inventory manager, one type of job appears inherently more flexible than the other. The important aspect is how the leader in that role views the job. The captain of the fire station could have approached his job in a very rigid manner and not responded to his community's needs in an effective way. By the same token, Helen was able to take control of her environment and institute important changes that strengthened her team. By looking at their particular job more broadly, leaders solve more problems, face more situations, and see the consequences of more actions. In the long run, developing a job so that it is unstructured may prove difficult; however, in the long run the payoff is more flexibility and opportunity to build problem-solving skills.

Building resilience in organizations

LEARNING FROM CULTURE IN EXTREME CONTEXTS

Nate Allen, at the time a major in the US Army, undertook an unconventional research project. Then again, Allen is no conventional army officer. Allen has proven that being unconventional, even within a traditional hierarchy like the US Army, led to extensive learning. One of his first breakthrough projects came as a young professor at the Military Academy at West Point, a key training ground for US Army officers. He and a group of unconventional thinking professors/officers, including Tony Burgess and Pete Kilner, sought a better way for officers to communicate across the world. The idea blossomed one day as Nate and Tony sat on a front porch. They wondered how to bring this informal conversation they were having face to face and share it with other officers. The problem was that these fellow officers were dispersed across the globe. They decided to try a new technology, the online forum. The idea of "CompanyCommander.com" was born (Dixson, Allen, Burgess, Kilner, and Schweiter, 2005). At the time, few had heard of an online professional forum. The technology was in its infancy. Today, tens of thousands of professional soldiers log online to professional forums like CompanyCommander.com and Platoonleader. com. The online electronic forum brought together officers across the globe to share stories, seek advice, and build the profession of soldiers nearly a decade before online forums like Facebook and Twitter would capture the attention of people around the world.

The result of their work put informal learning at the center of developing emerging leaders in the US Army. The online forums were built upon the idea that peers could teach each other in informal settings—a notion called peer-to-peer learning. *Harvard Business Review* (2006), one of the top journals of leadership practice in world, recognized the innovation as one of the "breakthrough ideas" in business leadership.

Moving a project from an idea born on a front porch into action and watching it flourish as a key source of learning in the US Army might stand as its own story on resilience. Where others may have seen barriers posed by hierarchy, technology, or knowledge, this group of young officers saw only an opportunity to build their profession by connecting soldiers online. Nate Allen undertook another unconventional project, one that put learning yet again at the forefront. This time, Allen put himself in the center of combat in Iraq to see how new officers were learning.

Allen wanted to learn how new leaders learned and developed in the face of the unprecedented conflict in Iraq. He wondered what these leaders were learning, how they were learning, and what skills they needed to be successful. He believed that this research might help other leaders learn in crisis situations, such as firefighters, police officers, emergency medical professionals, and even some types of executives. At the time, most of the research he read focused on how people *should* act in a crisis. In other words, most research focused on what leaders should *do* in a crisis, but not how they *learn* in the middle of a crisis. In order to find out how leaders learn, he took his research to a real crisis—frontline combat soldiers working in a war zone—where he conducted a series of intense interviews with US Army officers in Iraq. Specifically, his interviews captured how leaders learned and how they developed their leadership experiences. Even more importantly, he studied how these leaders developed leadership capacity in others. His interviews with commanders yielded some impressive, if not surprising, insights into learning-directed leadership. The learning process proved complex and rich.

The research interviews often took place in the middle of an ongoing war. In many cases, participants were interviewed just hours after engaging in hostile combat or within a few days of losing a valuable soldier to enemy fire. This led Allen to describe the environment as "molten," like hot lava exploding from a mountain. The term *molten* adds another layer to the rather dry description we have provided of leaders' context being complex and novel. Working successfully in this molten environment requires constant fast-paced learning and adaptation.

Three characteristics of the learning experience emerged. First, the learning experience involved gaining a sense of responsibility. Leaders weren't going through the motions, nor were they simply playing by the book. Leadership involved an emotional and cognitive engagement, a feeling of selflessness, and, most important, a strong sense of individual power and influence on situations and their outcomes. The leaders felt that the actions they took and the decisions they made had consequences. Leadership was no longer something abstract. Leadership was now a *profound responsibility*. The emotions that came with leadership were often invoked by direct feedback from the situation. The feedback was not superficial or inconsequential. The feedback was felt so deeply and intensely that Allen described it as *embodied feedback*. Related to the emotional intensity of the feedback, the leaders felt *intense affect*. Many of the leaders searched for ways to describe the deep emotions they felt for their troops. They used words like rage, anger, fear, joy, and relief (Allen and Kayes, 2010, p. 8).

Allen, now both a PhD in management and a colonel in the army, concluded his study by identifying four qualities that these commanders were learning: judgment, innovation, compassion, and resilience. Judgment resulted in the ability to take informed, but timely and consequential action. Judgment involved understanding organizational politics and navigating local power dynamics. Innovation required moving beyond existing methods, procedures, or protocols to accomplish goals. Compassion involved understanding the emotional side of a situation and being able to identify and at times manage the emotions of others. Resilience involved continued action and fulfillment of duties in the face of challenges unimaginable to most leaders. Figure 17 shows the culture of leadership in this context.

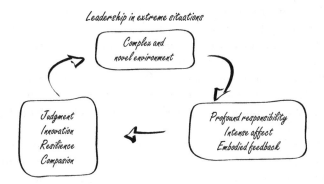

Figure 17 **Learning in combat**

DEVELOPING THE "MAXIMIZED VERTICAL RECONNAISSANCE ATTACK PROFILE"

Although Allen recounted many stories that demonstrate qualities of leadership, one in particular captured our attention: the story of going from horizontal to vertical.

"You won't see or hear us, but we'll be there," the helicopter pilot assured the troops on the ground. It was the dark of night over the Iraqi city, and the commander flew his helicopter at just the right altitude so that those on the ground could not hear it. All around the city, insurgents began lighting tires at nearly every street corner in order to ambush the ground crew. The pilot engaged his new strategy: he locked onto the enemy and dove his helicopter straight at the enemy, engaging his hellfire missile in descent. The strategy worked; he surprised the enemy, and the ground troops escaped unharmed. Over time, the strategy caught on and other pilots adopted the method, which was given a name only the military could come up with: "maximized vertical reconnaissance attack profile" (Allen, 2006, pp. 101–5).

One commander in Allen's study, the pilot of this helicopter, described his frustration with existing protocol. He described the limitation of flying his helicopter over the urban terrain. The helicopter was designed for what he referred to as "horizontal" combat, combat with an enemy measured primarily in distance such as an open field where enemy tanks sat in open view. The machine was effective in this kind of open combat; the machine was designed and built for war with a Soviet-type enemy. In an urban environment, like combat in much of Iraq, the design proved less effective. In urban combat, he needed his helicopter to fly vertically, taking sharp vertical climbs over buildings with limited open spaces to maneuver.

But where the machine could not adapt, its pilot could adapt the machine. Working with various groups, including fellow pilots, government contractors, the manufacturer of the aircraft, and his commanding officer, the pilot devised a "vertical strategy," where he would fly the bird at higher altitude than normal and literally dive his aircraft at the enemy, firing missiles as he descended. After extensive testing during his off hours, the attack strategy was devised and now is an accepted protocol for urban combat.

The story of the vertical attack shows the incredible resilience being learned by leaders in the most trying of situations, as well as innovation as the pilot sought a new use of complex equipment, compassion for the soldiers, and judgment in how he applied this innovation. Each contributed to this leader's ability to adapt in the face of difficult circumstances.

BUILDING A CULTURE OF RESILIENCE

Just as leaders build their own capacity to adapt and flourish, they also need to build resilience in organizations. Leaders do this in a number of ways: (1) building a culture accepting of failure; (2) encouraging innovation; (3) facilitating social networks based on positive thought and action; (4) demonstrating a time orientation based on patience, focused on achievement over time; and (5) valuing the development of self and others.

Resilience and innovation often go hand in hand, as in the case of the vertical attack profile innovation. In many cases, leaders can foster resilience by building innovative cultures within their organization. Organizations that have rigid cultures, where people hide mistakes and do not trust others to openly talk about problems, fail the resilience test. Resilient organizations know how to deal with failure because failure is already part of their culture. Consider Sir James Dyson, the English industrial designer known for his invention, the Dyson vacuum cleaner. Sir Dyson was fixated on creating a vacuum cleaner that would not lose suction while it picked up dirt, and after many attempts he invented one successfully. He recounted an exacting 5,127 failures over 10 years to come up with a single design that worked (Salter, 2007). After no UK manufacturer would sell his first patented product, afraid perhaps of upsetting the market of traditional vacuum cleaners based on suctioning into a bag, Dyson started his own organization. Dyson products are now available in 39 different countries. Failure, it appears, served Sir Dyson well.

Similarly one satirical newspaper we read about, *The Onion*, undergoes a formidable amount of testing, reviewing, and discarding each week. *The Onion* relies on clever headlines to draw readers into its website. Each week it generates nearly 500 new headlines, of which less than 20 will be used. That means that over 200 percent of the work is discarded each week (Schultz, 2010). Similarly, novelist Scott Turow believed in his own ability to write successful, commercial books. Before publishing his first novel, he had four entire books rejected before his future bestseller, *Presumed Innocent*, was bought by a publisher (Rose and Turow, 2010).

These examples describe product innovations—vacuum cleaners, newspapers, and books. Another type of innovation can be found in a knowledge-based organization, a small secretarial college that transformed into a thriving university. Villa Julie College was founded in 1947 by the Sisters of Notre Dame de Namur on an 80-acre estate outside Baltimore Maryland in the United States. By the late 1960s the college had broken with the Catholic Church to transform itself into an independent college governed by a board of trustees, admitting males in 1972. By 1984, the college had become a four-year college, granting bachelor's degrees. The real growth occurred from 2000 onward when a new president, Dr. Kevin Manning, took the helm. President Manning and the vice president Dr. Paul Lack were determined to bring innovation and growth into the culture of the college. The adaptation of the college skyrocketed. From 2004 to 2008, the college built residential housing, transformed the student population from commuters to residents, became a university, and changed its name to Stevenson University. The new Stevenson University adopted the motto "For Living, For Learning." While many independent US colleges suffered from decreased admissions and loss of capital projects, Stevenson University expanded. It added a football team to round out its sports teams and continued to build and acquire land as it added new majors, programs, and student activities. All this activity was risky, and at times the infrastructure was outpaced by the growth, but the university prided itself on creating an entrepreneurial culture of "try it out" rather than "it can't be done," while involving many people in their process of change. Dr. Paul Lack, commented on this process of fast change and innovation by stating, "[T]his risk was somewhat minimized by having patience to do careful research and undertaking extensive involvement with diverse constituents." This is remarkable considering the criticisms of universities in general for their lack of necessary change. White and Weathersby (2005) in *The Learning Organization*, for instance, pointed out that most change in academic institutions is slow; universities are notorious for shunning rapid growth.

An important lesson can be learned from these examples. When organizations, or leaders, build mechanisms for failure and recovery into the system, they naturally build in resilience by setting expectations, building recovery plans, or more generally building a culture that tolerates less-than-perfect solutions and is willing to "try it out." Importantly, however, when there is a failure, it is used as a learning experience. Cannon and Edmundson (2005) offered an example of one of these mechanisms at work. In their research on resilient organizations, they discovered that United Parcel Service (UPS) schedules time each week for employees to discuss and receive feedback on potential failures. This scheduled time is about half an hour and provides a structured method to show that leadership values feedback on what the organization can do to improve and adapt and identify and learn from small failures before there is a large failure. Leaders can build this resilience in themselves and their organizations in a variety of ways. Another method of generating adaptation and recovery at work is by creating a culture or network of like-minded people.

USING NETWORKS AND APPRECIATIVE INQUIRY TO SUPPORT RESILIENCE

A study of 5,000 adults conducted by a UK-based not-for-profit organization, The Young Foundation, found that a person's well-being or adjustment is dependent on the happiness of those around them in their network. According to this study, the clusters of well-being at work occur because positive emotion spreads throughout social networks. It is not that like-minded individuals only associate with others of the same disposition and attitude, but that well-being spreads. The converse of this is that negativity spreads through social networks as well. Bouncing back and adapting in the face of adversity is contagious. But, then again, so is remaining mired in the misery of failure, setbacks, and crisis.

Based on decades of research, psychologists have promoted this sharing of positive thoughts and emotions in the discipline of positive psychology (see, for example, Seligman, 1990, 2002; Seligman and Csikszentmihalyi, 2000). David Cooperrider and Ronald Fry, consultants and professors at Case Western Reserve University in Cleveland, have developed an approach to resilience that builds on an organization's strengths, extending positive psychology to the practice of leadership (see, for example, Trosten-Bloom, Cooperrider, and Whitney, 2003; Fry, Barrett, Seiling, and Whitney, 2001). They believe that resilience comes from focusing not on organizational problems, but on the positive aspects of an organization. They pose a few simple questions in their consultancy: What gives this organization life? What is the purpose of this organization, and how can it be developed? Questions like these focus the members of the organization on the organization's purpose rather than its challenges.

Appreciative inquiry (AI) is a method that organizational development practitioners use to encourage a culture of networks where people look beyond problems and focus on what is going well in the organization. By focusing on success, AI builds networks of people that notice strengths and share success stories. The four steps commonly used in AI are discovery, dreaming, design, and destiny. The first step, discovery, is about identifying strengths in an organization such as job satisfaction and where things went well. The second step, dreaming, is about building on data gathered during the discovery phase to dream about what the organization could be capable of in the next five years or more. During the third step, design, employees craft a compelling vision that supports the organizational strengths. During the fourth step, destiny, employees plan on achieving the positive dreams of the organization. Assumptions around AI include that what we focus on becomes our reality and that the language that we use constructs our reality. Therefore, using the language of success and focusing on what can be increases the chances that an organization will promote a culture of strength. American Express is an example of an organization that successfully used AI to redefine its culture based on its strengths. Senior management was able to make some organizational changes based on what employees identified as the dreams for information technology investments, which translated AI into improved performance.

TAKING THE LONG-TERM VIEW OF ORGANIZATIONAL ACHIEVEMENT

While the future is important for resilience, through envisioning a better future using AI, the future is also important in goal orientation and achievement. Gert Hoefstede, a Dutch researcher, conducted widespread research on cultures and found that national culture influences our time orientation. In the United States, the United Kingdom, Australia, and East Africa, for example, goal achievement has a short-term orientation, while other countries such as China and Japan have a longer-term orientation. Countries such as Brazil and India fall somewhere in-between. Organizational cultures

---

Strategies for leaders

Appreciative Inquiry
To practice AI at work, you can use several strategies:

1. Focus on the strengths that people bring to your organization. List the unique talents, attributes, and skills that people you work with bring to the workplace. Share your observations around the strengths that people have.
2. Do not limit yourself to problem analysis but also include conversations around future possibilities. Move from only asking "What is wrong here?" to considering "What is right and how do we continue this?"
3. Involve others. Reconsider structure. If you have a highly authoritarian structure, how can you involve people in decision making and future planning?

Source: Adapted from Trosten-Bloom, Cooperrider, and Whitney, 2003.

often reflect the national culture, and so understanding the constraints of time orientation is useful. Culture is a descriptive term, which means that it describes the reality of an organization; it doesn't describe how an organization *should* be or whether employees *like* the reality of the organization. Understanding the time orientation of an organization's culture is useful in understanding what factors might promote or hinder resilience. A leader interested in the long-term orientation emphasizes persistence over time and personal adaptability, whereas a short-term-oriented leader emphasizes quick results and protection of one's turf.

Conclusion

Cognitive, physiological, and environmental factors contribute to a leader's ability to adapt in the face of adversity, stress, crisis, or error. Leaders' ability to bounce back after failure is dependent on their efficacy, perceived control, and past experience with failure. Building resilient organizations, the work of the leader, is about creating and sustaining a culture of innovation— helping employees see the positive, persist over time, and try out ideas, despite failure.

Questions for reflection

1. What has been your experience with failure? How did you respond effectively? What could you have done better after the failure?
2. How will you develop efficacy in yourself and others?
3. How can you apply the lessons learned about optimism and pessimism at work?
4. How do you include both a short-term results orientation and a long-term focus? How do you encourage this mindset in others?

6 Fostering Emotional Intelligence

Key ideas

▶ Leadership requires more than analytical skills; leadership requires emotional intelligence—understanding and managing the emotions of self and others.

▶ Emotional intelligence involves self-awareness, self-management, social awareness, and relationship management.

▶ Learning-directed leaders understand the importance of emotional intelligence in self and others.

▶ A key element to developing emotional intelligence is motivation to learn.

This chapter describes the role of emotions in learning, how to harness the power of emotions to learn more effectively, and how to use emotions to meet new challenges. As leaders develop awareness of their own emotions, they enable followers to achieve greater self and social awareness. Research reveals that cognitive ability is not as important to leadership success as was once thought. Rather, success as a leader lies in the motivation to learn, the drive to acquire new skills, the development of emotional self-awareness and control, and the ability to read and influence the emotions of others.

A leader's story: Carl's risk at Morrison & Foerster law firm

Carl, then a managing partner for the law firm Morrison & Foerster, went to the University of Chicago Law School to recruit second-year law students for summer intern positions. At that time, Morrison & Foerster, based in San Francisco, had 175 lawyers and offices in Los Angeles, Denver, Washington, DC, and London. Today, the firm has 950 lawyers and 19 offices, including offices throughout Asia. Even in those days, the firm had a strategic interest in Asia, especially China and Japan, and that may have been what attracted Ken to sign up for an interview.

Having interviewed literally hundreds of law students at law schools such as Chicago, Michigan, Northwestern, Hastings, Stanford, and Berkeley, Carl had learned how difficult it is to determine in a 30-minute interview whether a student would ultimately become a strong partner at the firm, let alone make a serious difference in the firm's success. But offering Ken Siegel a summer internship was an easy decision. Ken was a bright, personable, poised young man with excellent academic credentials and a passion for international business. What Carl did not know is what an incredible impact Ken would have on the direction of Morrison & Foerster's international practice.

Ken did very well in his summer at the firm; so Carl and the partnership offered him a job as an associate after his graduation. Carl personally called him numerous times at his home in Chicago during his final months in school, but it seemed that Ken was trying to evade acceptance of this once-in-a-lifetime offer. In one of the calls, however, Carl began to understand Ken's position. What Ken really wanted was to take a year-long course in Japanese at Stanford's language program in Tokyo. Ken was engaged to a Japanese national. Carl knew that even his prime offer at Morrison & Foerster couldn't compete with young love. He quickly decided to make Ken an offer he couldn't refuse: the firm would pay his tuition and living expenses in Tokyo if he would commit now to join the firm on completion of the course. "I think this caught him off guard," Carl remembered, "because when I said, 'So, do we have a deal?' he simply said, 'OK.'" Carl had no idea whether his "deal" with Ken would even meet the approval of the firm, but he thought, "In this case it was better to ask forgiveness than permission." Armed with his understanding of contract law, and understanding his role as partner in the firm, he knew that he had bound the firm so the deal couldn't be reversed.

In September 1987, the firm opened its first Tokyo office with one partner and one associate. The associate was Ken Siegel. The firm had learned from its other international office experiences that it was one thing for an associate to have good law school grades, do good research for partners, and have an interest in living abroad, but it was another thing for the young lawyer to survive in a foreign environment. That takes a certain amount of what the firm called "peasant cunning." To find out the difference required putting the person on the ground overseas and hoping for the best.

Two months later, Carl saw Ken's "peasant cunning" in action. By now Carl had become the chairman of the firm, and he was present for the official opening of the Tokyo office in the fall of 1987. The reception was followed by a weekend where the Pac-Ten Conference held its annual overseas football game at the Tokyo Bowl. California was to play Washington State in the game, so the firm decided to make the game part of its opening celebration. They invited over 130 Japanese business clients and friends to the game but had not planned on how cold it can get in Tokyo in the fall. That morning there was a bit of panic in the little office. The scenario: Over 130 Japanese clients and friends facing the prospect of sitting for over 3 hours in the freezing cold watching a game they knew almost nothing about. This is where Ken's peasant cunning came into play.

He went to work on the telephone (using his newly acquired skill in Japanese) and rented 130 wool blankets. "To this day I don't know where he found them!" Carl recalled in amazement. Then there was the problem of getting 130 blankets to the stadium. By this time, Carl and the other visiting partners had left for the Tokyo Bowl to greet the guests. When they arrived, a long line of taxis pulled up in front of the stadium. Ken jumped out of the lead taxi and began the process of unloading piles of wool blankets from each taxi as it pulled up. He then arranged the distribution of the blankets to the guests with perfectly gracious Japanese introductions complete with low bows. Carl's faith and trust in Ken was sealed. "It was then that I knew our Tokyo venture was in good hands," he said.

The Tokyo office of Morrison & Foerster celebrated its twentieth anniversary in September 2007. The office now has over 90 lawyers, one of the largest law offices in Japan. And the managing partner of the office is none other than Mr. Peasant Cunning—Siegel San!

Carl and his protégé demonstrate a key attribute of learning-directed leadership called emotional intelligence. Emotional intelligence, or EI, describes the willingness and ability to understand people. EI moves the leader beyond pure analytical reasoning. Carl understood the deeper motivation of his future employee when he realized that love doesn't take a back seat to a career, even among those with high achievement orientation. At the same time, Ken demonstrated the ability to understand the Japanese culture in a way that others in his firm could not.

The story of Ken and Carl demonstrates another, equally important, reason that EI is gaining attention: A connection exists between the EI of leaders and organizational outcomes. Studies report that EI, the ability to understand and influence others, accounts for more than 60 percent of performance and matters almost twice as much as cognitive intelligence or technical competency (Robbins, 2007). Further, research links EI to financial growth, market reputation, project management success (Clarke, 2010), job satisfaction, and worker commitment (Chi-sum, Ping-man, and Peng, 2010).

The practical science of emotions

The popular press has also caught on to the appeal of EI. A *Time* magazine cover story focused on how EI was redefining what it means to be smart. Intelligence goes far beyond analytical reasoning ability and even critical thinking to encompass how an individual motivates self and others, taking into account emotions and values. *Scientific American's Mind* magazine devoted a section in September 2008 to "The Expert Mind." They concluded that motivation to learn is critical to success and more critical to success than innate ability. Highly successful athletes, grandmasters in chess, and others are the result of motivation and training, not ability. Motivation to learn involves persisting in the face of setbacks and failure, searching out challenging opportunities, and striving for personal development.

For many years, ideas of intelligence focused on a narrow set of criteria such as performance on an IQ, SAT, or similar test of cognitive ability. This narrow focus occurred for some good reasons. Standard intelligence tends to solidify at a young age and changes very little over time. Research presents conflicting explanations as to exactly why cognitive intelligence stabilizes like this. Some believe that IQ is genetic, while others believe it is a factor of socioeconomic class. Only within the last few decades has the idea of an alternative to cognitive intelligence been taken seriously. Standard definitions dominate our understanding of intelligence for another reason as well. IQ and SAT tests provide an easy and inexpensive means to measure intelligence using simple pen and paper. Because organizations have accumulated millions of scores over many decades, a statistically accurate sample of distributions of these scores is readily available. Nevertheless, many are beginning to question the value of these tests and take notice of an alternative, EI (Gibbs et al., 1995).

The concept of EI began with Thorndike (1920), an early psychologist, and his concept of social intelligence. He described social intelligence along three dimensions: (1) abstract intelligence, or the ability to grasp and manage ideas; (2) mechanical intelligence, or the ability to perceive concrete objects; and (3) social intelligence, or the ability to understand and manage people. Harvard professor Howard Gardner (1983) extended this thinking by identifying nine different intelligences (he later went on to add a few more). In particular, he argued that there is an interpersonal intelligence and intrapersonal intelligence. Interpersonal, or social, intelligence results in the ability to understand and relate to other people, whereas intrapersonal intelligence results in the ability to understand the self (see Figure 18).

Salovey and Mayer (1990) have served as leaders in the systematic study of EI, which they define as "the subset of social intelligence that involves

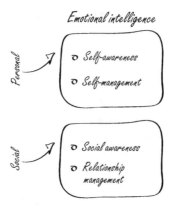

Figure 18 **Two dimensions of emotional intelligence**

the ability to monitor one's own and others' feelings and emotions" (p. 189). This includes the ability to generate certain emotions, perceive emotions, and use awareness of one's own emotions in order to regulate emotions (Mayer and Salovey, 1997). Mayer and Salovey's research made strides in developing a systematic research-based model of EI.

Where Mayer and Salovey focused mainly on abilities, Boyatzis and Goleman focused on competencies in leadership settings. Goleman, Boyatzis, and McKee (2002) have not only popularized the term EI, but have made the concept applicable to leaders. They link EI to various work outcomes and leadership competencies. A competency, according to Boyatzis (2009), is a capability or ability that results from intended behaviors. EI competencies include an amalgamation of emotional, social, and cognitive abilities. They summarize EI to include self-awareness and self-management, which is built upon emotional data about oneself; social intelligence, which relies on understanding and using emotional data about others; and cognitive intelligence, which focuses on analyzing the data that causes optimal performance (Boyatzis, 2009).

Emotional intelligence as learning

Even more crucial, although IQ cannot generally be improved, EI can be learned. Leaders learn EI through experience and specialized training, but both require motivation to improve. Unlike general intelligence, EI usually improves with age. Life experience itself may improve EI, but targeted training and development activities can lead to more effective interpretation and regulation of emotion.

"Steven," a composite character that symbolizes many managers that we work with, serves as a powerful example of learning EI. A database administrator, Steven attended a leadership workshop, that we led, for rising supervisors. In this workshop, he learned about the importance of reaching out to people and building a network. Steven valued these skills. He had always been more comfortable behind a computer than approaching and having what felt like "forced conversations" with coworkers. Steven was aware that he needed to improve these skills, but awareness in itself wasn't sufficient. To build social skills, Steven needed to be motivated to change, to do something different than he had been doing. A training and development approach that focused on EI could help. The program included a 360-degree feedback survey where Steven's peers, supervisors, and employees commented on his EI. Steven completed an assessment of his emotional intelligence competencies, the same evaluation form that his boss, employees and peers filled out about him and then compared his scores to those where others evaluated him. He compared what he thought his strengths and weaknesses were with what others perceived his strengths and weaknesses and looked for areas where everyone was in agreement and areas where his assessment was out of alignment with the assessment made by others.

In addition to attending training sessions, Steven recently found a coach to help enable his growth. Together, they worked on building general skills, such as recognizing emotions in others. They also reviewed specific situations. For example, they discussed an incident where Steven and another manager had a significant disagreement. Steven stormed off and found himself unable to concentrate for the rest of the day, distracted by the episode and his reaction. The coach also helped him overcome his anxiety in building his social network, reaching out to new people, and strengthening relationships with existing colleagues and associates. The coach helped Steven reflect on his emotions and behaviors, and they discussed how he could become more productive and continue to gain momentum with network building, even after discontinuing his meetings with the coach. Steven's experience highlights the importance of emotional intelligence with the work of the leader. Emotional intelligence has multiple components that can be examined in its entirety and as a separate set of dimensions.

Dimensions of emotional intelligence

Collaborators at the Consortium for Research on Emotional Intelligence in Organizations (http://www.eiconsortium.org) generally agree that EI consists of four dimensions: self-awareness, self-management, social awareness, and relationship management (see Table 5).

120

Table 5 **Emotional intelligence competencies**

Dimension	Competencies	What this looks like...
Self-awareness	• Emotional self-awareness: being in tune with your emotions • Accurate self-assessment: understanding your strengths and weaknesses • Self-confidence: Knowing your capabilities	• Understanding the connection between what you feel, do, and say • Knowing what your values and goals are • Recognizing the emotions you experience
Self-management	• Emotional self-control • Transparency • Adaptability • Achievement • Initiative: acting on opportunities • Optimism	• Keeping negative emotions and urges in check • Being consistent and trustworthy • Showing flexibility in a changing environment • Improving and meeting high levels of excellence • Looking at the positive side of events
Social awareness	• Empathy: understanding others' emotions, perspectives, and interests • Organizational awareness: understanding the politics in an organization • Service: identifying and delivering on stakeholder needs	• Listening to others • Showing sensitivity to social cues • Understanding social networks • Understanding the perspective of other stakeholders
Relationship management	• Inspirational leadership: leading with a vision • Influence: using persuasion to get things done • Development of others: focusing on others' competencies • Change catalyst: leading and managing in a new direction • Conflict management: resolving conflicts • Building bonds: strengthening relationships with others • Teamwork and collaboration: team building	• Being skilled at persuading others • Providing open communication • Leading by example • Focusing on building strengths in followers • Changing the status quo • Building networks • Building team learning

Source: Goleman, Boyatzis, and McKee, 2002.

SELF-AWARENESS

As a full-time manager of a not-for-profit organization as well as a part-time graduate student, "Marissa" began to reflect on her leadership abilities and how she could learn to more effectively influence others. She began maintaining a journal each night as part of a leadership development course she was taking. She hoped that through journaling, she would develop a better understanding of her strengths, weaknesses, values, emotional triggers, and behavior. The journal provided a psychologically safe and non-threatening method for self-learning.

In addition to her leadership journal, she was assigned a peer mentor, "Liz," as part of this class. Marissa trusted Liz. Although they did not work in the same organization, they shared many common experiences. Marissa also liked Liz because she was objective and wasn't afraid to say what she felt, but was considerate of how her feedback would be received. Over the course of the semester, Marissa began to share her journal entries with Liz, which proved to be an important source of learning.

The journal experience was helpful to Marissa, and she continued to write once the class was completed. She began to try different forms of expression and learning. She began writing a blog, a personal journal entry, and an email to her trusted mentor or a public post on her social media account. Marissa had found that writing was a great source of learning about herself and the leader she was becoming. She wrote:

> Today I addressed the project leader's poor performance as it related to a specific deliverable he provided to me. As the first conversation I've ever had with a superior regarding their lack of understanding of the task and unacceptable results, I would say I did a fine job. I think I could have approached the subject more delicately, but that would not be a true reflection of my personality to do so.
> . . . The project leader became defensive and physically agitated. He raised his voice and in response, I did the same. He doled out several subjective criticisms of my work product.
> ("Marisa," MBA student, as cited in Kayes, A. B., 2008)

Marissa's journal entry provides an example of how self-awareness involves being in tune with emotions. Importantly, self-awareness must be accurate; it involves understanding how others perceive your strengths, weaknesses, capabilities, and limitations. Self-awareness is the foundation for the other EI competencies as well. Failure to accurately assess your emotions and how these emotions interact with your vision and goals means you will never be able to manage them. Understanding yourself takes time and patience, and a bit of courage. Marissa's story highlights a number of successful strategies that she used for improving self-awareness:

▶ Identify your personal values and their impact at work
▶ Identify what triggers stress and how you behave in stressful situations
▶ Identify the causes and consequences of your emotions and mood

Leaders who focus on self-awareness focus on learning about themselves. Once they learn more about themselves, they can begin to identify and develop strategies to cope in new situations. Research shows that self-awareness matters for leaders at *all* levels of an organization. In health services, for instance, the CEOs in the best-performing companies had the highest self-awareness; those CEOs with the lowest self-awareness had the poorest performing companies (Goleman, Boyatzis, and McKee, 2002). Emerging leaders, such as Marissa, realize the importance of self-awareness too. Using her journal as the basis for improving self-awareness, however, Marissa discovered that self-awareness in itself wasn't enough to improve her leadership. Self-awareness improved her understanding of her own emotions and solidified her values, but she wanted to take another step. Marissa wanted to put her values into action. She needed to practice better self-management.

SELF-MANAGEMENT

Marissa sought to improve her ability to own her emotions. We often see examples of ineffective management of emotions in our work and one example that comes to mind is the management of workplace anger. A 1996 Gallup poll showed that one in four employees dealt with significant and constant workplace anger. This anger manifests itself in inappropriate behaviors from both employees and management. One skill of EI, involves identifying these negative emotions like anger and keeping them in check.

Managing negative emotions, however, is only part of self-control; in some cases, leaders may fail to take any action. Anger in the workplace is a failure of self-management—the inability to manage negative emotions. Self-management requires taking action toward a goal despite feelings of fear and anger. One of our students provides an example of how negative emotions can limit learning about leadership. For class, she was assigned to read an article that reported tables of graduate-level research statistics.

Strategies for leaders

▶ Know what you value and on which values you place the most importance. What are the top three values that you bring to the workplace? How do you live these values at work?

▶ Understand how you react under pressure. If you are generally level headed, do you become prone to outbursts of frustration?

▶ Acknowledge the relationship between your moods and work. What times of day are you in your best mood and worst mood? What time of day are you most productive? What other activities might trigger moods (such as work, home, meetings, travel)?

▶ Recognize people that can provide feedback to balance the accuracy of your self-assessment. What people that you interact with could help you analyze your self-awareness around emotion?

When she saw the numbers, she froze. She commented that the article was too hard, that she was "not good at math." This deeply rooted emotion about her math competence prevented her from learning. She felt that she had never been good at math, even though her grades in math were always high. She recounted an experience of taking a math test years ago as an undergraduate student. Anticipation of the upcoming test, she recalled, made her physically ill. Her heart rate accelerated. She perspired and went into a state of near panic. All of this was motivated by her negative emotions about math. Years later, when confronted with this article in a class that contained statistics, these old emotions resurfaced again.

Unfortunately, many of our formal learning experiences mirror this student's experience. Formal learning, from kindergarten through graduate education, too often relies on punishment and rewards, rather than intrinsic motivation. Organizational culture and politics only contribute to the negative emotions often associated with learning. McCracken's study (2005) described how organizations use formal learning activities as forms of punishment and reward rather than to encourage actual learning. For example, some organizations rely on leadership development classes to improve poor performance or reward higher performers with off-site retreats billed as leadership development. In other cases, learning activities are obligations, where employees simply check the box in order to move on to the next assignment. Negative emotions often result from this flawed punishment and reward mentality. According to McCracken, a culture emerges where organizations view learning as obligatory and not fundamentally necessary. Further, the bigger message that employees receive is that learning occurs only in a classroom. Perhaps the worst result from this situation is a culture that tells employees not to try anything new since they may fail because the company hasn't built a culture of learning and development.

In summary, institutions as well as leaders must continually battle the negative emotions often associated with learning. Despite the barriers and the forces against learning, leaders need to continually develop skills to fight these negative emotions. Self-management sits at the core of interacting with others. The next dimension of EI lies in being aware of others, the dimension of emotional social awareness.

SOCIAL AWARENESS

Social awareness, the third dimension in Goleman and Boyatzis's model of EI, engages both a concern for self as well as a focus on others. An

---

Strategies for leaders

▶ Learn to apply the mind-body connection. Incorporate physical activity: yoga, walking, swimming, biking, or another activity. Regular physical activity can reduce stress, increase your oxygen intake, and clear your mind from immediate or nagging negative emotions.

▶ Decide to wait for a period of time before reacting to something. Don't be shackled to impulse. If you are angered by something at work, delay sending that e-mail for 24 hours.

▶ Identify barriers that hold you back in various situations or reduce your motivation and set a goal to conquer one or more at a time. Is there something that you do not like to do but know it would be a good skill? If you feel anxiety every time you have to speak in public, for example, volunteer to lead the next meeting. Over time, your skill will improve and you will have conquered this barrier.

▶ Look for success. Seek out examples of people and situations that display successful management of emotion. It can be easy to find negative examples, but practice observing positive examples and learn from them. Perhaps one of these people who has mastered self-management could be your mentor.

important element of social awareness is empathy—an understanding of others' emotions, perspectives, and interests. Empathy is not feeling sorry for others, but understanding people and their world. Social awareness also includes a leader's ability to read the unique needs of various stakeholders in the organization and to consider their interests in the context of the politics of the organization.

Not too long ago, Harvard Medical School realized the power of empathy in patient care and decided to revise its medical school curriculum. Educators based the revision on more than a hunch. They were motivated by a number of research studies that highlighted an important problem. Developing empathy for patients was an important part of medical practice; it even improved diagnosis, cures, and patient satisfaction. Yet empathy was not taught as a skill in medical education (Hojat et al., 2004). In fact, Hojat and colleagues found that the traditional process of educating students at many medical schools actually reduced empathy. Further, studies showed that physicians scored poorly on tests to identify and match emotion with facial expression (Hojat et al., 2005). Harvard Medical School responded to this dismal trend with some radical changes to the curriculum of its medical residency program, which continues physicians' training after medical school.

The program encouraged the young physicians to consider a broader range of factors in determining care, such as a patient's lifestyle, culture, social class, and other factors pertinent to his or her unique situation. They also considered ethical issues and the ability of the patient to communicate. Students engaged in elaborate role-plays, where a mock patient might mention having to sleep upright in a chair and how that led to a loss of work as an auto mechanic. The patient might also mention that he missed picking up and hugging his two-year-old daughter. The role of the physician was to understand the entire patient as a worker and as a father. Ultimately, this improved the patients' prospects for care and the residents' training and development. With the new changes in curriculum, residents not only followed senior physicians to learn from them in their interactions with patients, but also followed patients. Understanding what patients struggled with, whether it was pain or paperwork, enabled these young physicians to empathize—see the world through the eyes of the patient.

Another element of social awareness focuses on grasping the realities of organizational politics and the unique needs of multiple internal and external stakeholders. This broad understanding is referred to as organizational awareness. By watching and listening to people and interacting with them, leaders will develop a deeper understanding of the needs and emotions of others, even when they drastically differ from their own. However, this too is a learned skill. Awareness of self and others serves as the foundation of learning EI, but EI is not limited to awareness.

Leaders need to transform awareness into skills. Putting awareness into action requires learning relationship management skills.

RELATIONSHIP MANAGEMENT

Technical competence and organizational loyalty served leaders well. Companies such as Air Canada, Deloitte, American Express, L'Oreal Cosmetics, and even the US Air Force test for EI (McGinn, 2007; Spencer and Spencer, 1993). Air Canada uses an EI Inventory to test new pilots because they found that airline captains need high levels of EI to serve as leaders in the cockpit. Captain Dave Legge, vice president of flight operations, advocated for the use of an EI assessment and its importance as a predictor of leadership ability. He said,

> An airline captain is, if you want to look at it in a certain way, a team leader. He's overseeing the cockpit crew, the flight crew as well as the cabin crew. And he is not only interacting with the other crewmembers but also with other departments within the airline. Obviously if you have to interact well with other people, these are instruments that we can use during the selection process to identify people that have these enhanced skills.
>
> (McGinn, 2007, p. FW3)

Strategies for leaders

▶ Ask questions instead of always providing the answers.
▶ Learn to read nonverbal as well as verbal cues. To accurately gauge the social and behavioral context, nonverbal signal reading is essential. Can you identify when one of your peers is anxious? Are you able to accurately assess why a customer of your organization is quieter than usual?
▶ Learn about other cultures and cultural differences in communication.
▶ Keep track of networks in your organization, identifying informal leaders and key sources of information. Know those people in your network who will help bring you to a higher level of job performance.

Relationship management involves learning a variety of skills, as Captain Legg noted. Coalition building, which includes building and maintaining a network of people, lies at the heart of applying EI with others. Coalitions are brought together to support an idea or common cause. Social network analysis provides a tool for leaders to determine how expansive their network is. Through this network, coalitions can be formed and managed. The social networks of an individual are useful to understand for this purpose, but what about all the networks of all employees in one organization? Social network analysis is the formal method used to map and identify networks visually for a number of uses. Individuals can utilize this tool to find their pockets of influence and assess the depth and breadth of their relationships, and organizations can also utilize this tool at a macro level. At a macro level, organizations identify areas that are on the fringe of information and those that are the hubs of information. Organizations can utilize network analysis to see where pockets of knowledge are dispersed, where workers share informal knowledge and information, and gaps in the formal design structure of the organization promote barriers to information.

Some firms (Rush, 2002) map the people networks within and across teams both qualitatively through interviews and quantitatively through assessment. The density and frequency of social networks can be identified through interviews and mapped using software. Questions such as "Who do you talk to?" and "Who do you go to for help?" assisted in establishing who was interacting in the organization. Then, the information is represented on a visual map to show the informal organization, with dark patches representing patterns of interactions and light patches showing where there is little interaction. Networks that are dense and knowledge-rich could be studied, rewarded, and replicated.

Rob Cross, a University of Virginia professor, led similar studies at companies such as Microsoft and Pfizer. In his research, he wasn't interested in general patterns of knowledge sharing, but rather in patterns that led to higher performance. He asked questions such as "Who helps you to perform better?" Two thirds of the people that were critical to the success of the organization were not on the organization's formal list of high performers (Dvorak, 2009). Figure 19 shows an example of what an individual's social network might look like.

It is important for leaders to understand (1) if their personal networks consist of those people who can help them perform better and (2) if those people that help the organization perform better. These people should be retained and rewarded. For management of relationships in EI, Dr. Cross's approach, focusing on those coalitions that drive higher performance, seems to be a pragmatic approach to networks. After all,

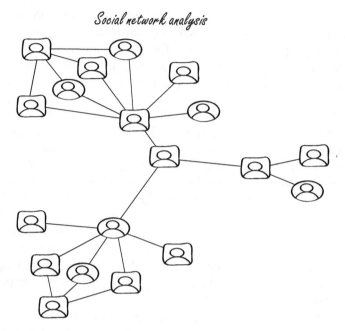

Figure 19 **Social network analysis**

Strategies for leaders

▶ Understanding is a step in the direction of effectively managing encounters and relationships with others. Build your understanding of others by branching out in your professional and personal relationships.

▶ Don't just analyze your network, practice building your network. Identify who you know in your organization and how you can improve your relationships. Cultivate these relationships and determine additional relationships that you would like to build within and outside of your organization.

▶ Identify who you know in your community—coworkers from previous positions, friends, relatives, and business contacts—and strengthen those relationships. Find how you can improve your job performance based on these relationships.

simply managing relationships to build depth and breadth in a network is a starting point, but managing those relationships that translate to improved performance at work is even better. As with any leadership competency, ethical considerations affect how and for what purpose a competency is employed.

The real rewards of emotional intelligence—more ethical leadership

EI plays a critical role in leadership. It paves the way for more positive interactions between the leader and those being led. In Western countries, our analytically based cultures often discount the role of emotion in decision-making. Hopes, fears, dreams, and ambition propel leaders toward action, plowing over values and principles. But not all situations can be understood from a purely rational perspective. Data do not always provide the answer. What may be needed to improve ethical decision-making is a better understanding of emotional impulses and how goals are often achieved at the expense of what is right. EI comes into play as a means to increase awareness and help regulate these impulses and improve decision-making. Carol Gilligan (1982), a Harvard-based psychologist, advocates for an ethical perspective based on compassion in addition to one based on analytics. Gilligan's vision is achieved only when leaders improve their EI and expand their interactions to include compassion as well as cognitive-based interactions.

Research supports the position that EI can lead to greater ethical behavior (Joseph, Berry, and Deshpande, 2009). Leaders with high levels of EI are less likely to justify their own unethical behavior by referring to the unethical behavior of others. They set their own course based on standards, not by simply following the crowd. This is a compelling case for development of EI in leaders, because research also shows that behavior is learned from others in the workplace. Coworkers and peers have a significant impact on behavior; ethical misconduct by others promotes more ethical misconduct. This is called social learning theory, the idea that people model and learn from others. Those with high levels of EI are better able to distinguish between a behavior to model and an inappropriate behavior.

The reason that EI may be lacking in some leaders may be due to the fact that most management training programs, including MBA, fail to adequately emphasize the use of emotions. Business education emphasizes cognition and minimizes the role of emotions (Holian, 2006). Colleges and universities socialize students into becoming critical thinkers who value rationality and logic. These are valuable skills, but unfortunately students often acquire these more cognitive skills at the expense of learning EI. Balancing cognitive values with EI before students enter the workforce may lead to better ethical decision-making at work (Holian, 2006).

"Stephanie," a consultant who worked as an auditor for an international accounting firm, explained the importance of EI to learning about ethics in the workplace.

> Role modeling behavior is essential as an auditor. You have to under-stand your own emotional impulses and the impulses of your clients. Sometimes, I just wanted to finish the audit; I was tired, frustrated, and had a million other things to work on. But, I controlled these feelings and kept with the audit. This motivation was contagious. I learned so much by sticking with some of the most frustrating situations at client organizations. Also contagious was admitting my mistakes. This helped my credibility! I was able to show that it is okay to make a mistake and talk about it. This helped with my colleagues so we could share lessons learned from our clients, and this helped with clients who were more willing to share their own mistakes. I think that if you don't recognize and understand your clients' impulses and mistakes, you help to let an unethical climate persist.

Stephanie's story illustrates how her emotional intelligence competencies impact others' ethical choices while improving decision-making. Creating an environment where clients could learn rather than a climate where clients had to cover their mistakes was a positive and useful step in building organizational ethics.

Conclusion

Leaders who learn to harness their own emotions, challenge their emotional fears, and break down institutional barriers that block learning will benefit themselves and their organizations. Overcoming frustration, expressing negative emotions in a diplomatic way, and being conscious of others' emotions build credibility. Effective self-management contributes to consistency and trustworthiness so leaders can have a greater impact. Building and managing these relationships is an ongoing process of learning. Emotional intelligence is at the heart of learning—it leads to better communication, it spurs motivation and perseverance to learn.

Questions for reflection

1. How important is emotional intelligence in my workplace? What are some organizational mechanisms that support emotional intelligence? (e.g., do we hire people who are strong in these competencies? Do we reward people who demonstrate EI?)
2. Which of the emotional intelligence competencies represent my strengths? Which of these competencies are areas for me to work on?
3. How does ethical behavior relate to emotional intelligence in my organization?
4. How can I develop these emotional intelligence competencies in others?

7 Team Learning

Key ideas

▶ Leading teams involves building shared beliefs and team-learning behaviors.

▶ Team-learning behaviors include three interrelated processes: coordinating, continuously improving, and adapting.

▶ To foster team learning, leaders must work to establish an environment that engenders appropriate levels of control and participation.

▶ Team-learning processes track the experiential learning cycle and include building a shared purpose, reflective integration, critical conversations, and taking action.

▶ Team learning emerges as teams develop through five phases of a developmental process.

Achieving the learning advantage requires teamwork. Team learning marks a movement from individual learning to learning across individuals and serves as the basis for moving from individual to organizational learning. Even though team skills are among the top three qualities employers seek in their employees (National Association of Colleges and Employers, 2010), being an effective team member is difficult to master without support from a leader. In this chapter, we outline how leaders can draw on learning principles to build and sustain successful teams. Leaders build team-learning beliefs and behaviors, navigate the learning cycle, recognize and overcome barriers, and facilitate teams through a progression of phases that lead to high-performance learning.

A leader's story: Brian leads a television news crew at Bloomberg TV

Brian looked nervously at his watch. It was pouring rain outside. A live news feed was less than a minute away, but his guest was nowhere to be found. Brian and his newly formed team couldn't depend on happenstance to ensure the live feed actually happened. Success depended on learning.

Although Brian had arrived in Nashville, Tennessee, the night before, he had met his newly formed production crew just three hours ago. The team included an on-air reporter named Lindsey, a freelance production crew, hired locally, which included an audio expert, a person to control the camera, and a lighting expert. They came to report on the soon-to-be-concluding 2008 US presidential debate between Barack Obama and John McCain. The team would begin taping just after the debate ended. This is when the campaign managers and political analysts or "pundits" as they are called, began their "spin" or commentary on the debate. Brian anxiously awaited his on-air guest. The debate itself appeared on TV channels throughout the world, including Bloomberg TV. The channel took its name from its founder, Michael Bloomberg, a successful entrepreneur and currently the mayor of New York City. The growing company often relied on young and ambitious college graduates, like Brian to lead their productions. He was 24 years old. Even in his short time as producer, he had mastered the complex technical and logistical side of TV production, but for this shot to be a success, he needed to draw on an additional set of skills. He would need to build trust and lead the team effectively.

Brian needed to build trust beyond his immediate team as well: the line producer who sat in a dry and noisy room in downtown New York City needed the live feed shot on his monitor in less than 45 seconds to ensure continuity as the show switched from inside the debate hall to the outside reporter. With only 45 seconds to go, there was still no guest.

Despite the hectic pace, the team members remained confident they would be successful. The group of highly trained professionals had successfully pulled of live shots dozens of times. Other factors, however, threatened their production. Protestors, police, campus officials, and curious onlookers all could prove obstacles. As the team waited nervously under a leaking shelter, kludged together from items purchased from Home Depot just hours ago, rain poured in from every side. The day had moved so quickly that Brian had little time to digest each action. It was difficult to build a team when there was no time for building consensus. The luxury of getting input from each team member didn't exist. Yet the team worked without thinking about it, smoothly shifting between tasks. Team members performed each action on time, in sequence. As Brian later recalled, "there is no time to sugar coat words. I needed to express urgency and be forceful enough to be sure that things happened immediately." At the same time, he always knew not to "shout or make the team members cynical, or make anybody angry." At the same time, in a live situation like this, the broadcast culture accepts that "you might frustrate in the moment, but you can apologize later." Just 30 seconds before going live.

By this time, a makeshift city had emerged. News organizations from around the world descended on the southern town. The news crews were so tightly packed together, getting in and out from the tent required a strategic plan. Avoiding the downfall of rain appeared almost impossible. With just seconds to the live feed, Brian saw his guest just a few yards away. The only thing that lay between 15 seconds to live and empty airtime was film crews, cameras, tent stakes, and host of other reporters going live on camera. Brian watched in confidence as one of his crew ran to the out-of-breath guest. Then they ducked under a competitor's camera, dodged a reporter, avoided knocking over a tent, and leaped over a river of cords that covered the ground. "We go live in 3, 2, 1 . . ." said Brian. A shot of Lindsey standing next to the guest came through on television sets around the world. To the viewer at home, a seamless transition from inside the debate to the reporter under the tent occurred. Team learning and team leadership made the shot.

Team learning

The television news crew that effortlessly coordinated its actions, continually improved its process moving toward a common goal, and quickly adapting to outside changes represents the best of team learning (see Kayes, D. C. 2004, 2006b). In our decade-long research program, we have observed many teams like this news crew that has achieved great success. Many of the teams we've observed shared strong values. For example, team members often share a common goal and understand the need to support each other. In teams that learn, values alone were not sufficient. Our observation and research with hundreds of teams led us to the following conclusion: Team learning, not simply shared values, rests at the heart of successful team efforts, especially when teams face novel and complex situations. For teams to be effective, team members must not only share common values, but must coordinate actions across time and space and expertise.

Team learning describes how teams gather, distribute, coordinate, and share information related to their task. Team learning improves a team's capacity to deal effectively with internal and external demands. For example, many factors are outside the control of the news crew. These factors include terrain, weather, duration, and other factors, but the internal dynamics of teamwork serve as the foundation for learning. To understand why internal team dynamics are so important, we turn to the issue of control and participation in aircraft cockpit crews.

Control and participation

In 1954, the US Navy lost 776 aircrafts. Research showed that many of the losses occurred due to human error. In the US Marine Corps, for example, 50 percent of errors in the cockpit were skill based. In other words, about half of all the errors in Marine aviation resulted from human errors such as failure to follow proper procedures, flying the aircraft in an inappropriate way, or misreading the terrain. By the year 2000, the number of naval aircraft lost had fallen to 24. Technology advancements played an important part in improving aircraft safety. But something other than technology also played a critical role. In 1987, the Marine Corps began a comprehensive program of Crew Resource Management or CRM (Navy Aviation Schools Command, 2010a). CRM was different from traditional training because it didn't emphasize technical skills. Instead, this new form of training emphasized leadership skills. The training sought to help pilots understand, for example, how workload can affect judgment or how a breakdown in a crew's decision-making, communication, and planning might impact operational performance. Specifically, the Marine aviators would learn how to improve judgment, coordinate with other members of the crew, and improve psychological awareness of both the situation and the state of the crew itself. Since the introduction of CRM in aviation, many other industries have adopted this form of teamwork. US Marines, other branches of the military around the world, commercial pilots, surgical teams, and even workers in business organizations have adopted its basic formula. Many of the factors related to accidents cannot be changed, but there are always areas for improvement and learning.

One of the challenges of leading a team involves the degree to which a leader should express control and allow participation from other members. Learning-directed leaders consider the context in which they are leading and adapt to the situation. In some cases, when teams fail to function properly, when they face time-critical situations, or when they simply are in a state of conflict, a team leader may need to take a dominant role, telling the team exactly what to do. In other cases, however, team leaders consult with their team members, act as a guide and encourage maximum participation. Whether the situation calls for high control or high facilitation, team leaders employ certain tactics that facilitate learning.

The US Department of Homeland Security and other teams that rely on CRM have addressed the degree of assertiveness appropriate for leaders. If leaders demonstrate too much assertiveness, they are likely to limit participation and increase control. On the other hand, if they allow too much participation, they limit their own control and the situation can turn into a free-for-all. Most leaders seek a balance between participation and control. When leaders actively seek the input of others, stand ready to accept others' viewpoints, and set a tone where others feel they can provide input without fear of retribution, they achieve an appropriate level of control. Leaders can be too passive when they avoid conflict, appear disinterested, or fail to provide clear directions or to set a positive

Table 6 **The assertiveness continuum**

Passive	Assertive	Overaggressive
Is overly courteous	Is actively involved	Dominates
"Beats around the bush"	Is ready to take action	Intimidates
Avoids conflict	Provides useful information	Is abusive/hostile
Is "along for the ride"	Makes suggestions	Barks out orders

Source: Department of Homeland Security, Customs and Border Protection (Navy Aviation Schools Command, 2010b).

tone. Overly aggressive leaders intimidate others, act overly confident, express doubts about the contributions of others, or routinely take actions without consulting others. Table 6 shows the assertiveness continuum used during CRM training to help leaders seek the appropriate level of assertiveness.

Developing a group of individuals into a team

When a group of individuals comes together as a team, they share the potential to advance to a higher level of learning than that achieved by any one individual working alone. We want to emphasize that teams hold this *potential*. Too often teams stagnate rather than thrive. Team learning is not a given. Team learning is more likely to occur when teams deliberately seek out learning. When we discuss the section on navigating the learning cycle, this is explored in more detail. But, first, we need to look at the basics of becoming a team. Theodore Mills (1967), an early sociologist, proposed a way to understand how a group transforms into a team. We drew on this model to describe a five-phase process, where a collection of individuals can progress to a cohesive team (Kayes, Kayes, and Kolb, 2005). It is from the formation of the team that team learning can occur.

PHASE 1: IMMEDIATE GRATIFICATION OF INDIVIDUAL MEMBERS

In the first stage of becoming a team, team members' focus is simple: they seek to realize their own immediate goals. In fact, it is unlikely that the team members will feel part of a team at all. For example, a person might attend a music concert but have no plans on interacting with the audience or musicians again. The purpose of joining is simply to enjoy the concert. Most team members will have difficulty understanding why this situation has any bearing on teamwork at all, so in this phase the leader helps the individuals in the team understand the potential interdependencies of this ad hoc group.

PHASE 2: SUSTAINED CONDITIONS FOR GRATIFICATION

Individuals may believe that joining a team is more than simply a one-shot opportunity. They may see joining the team as a sustained effort with some benefits. The role of the learning-directed team leader is quite different than it is in phase 1. Here, the team leader needs to help the team members understand that in order to function over time, the team needs to set up formal and informal processes, norms, and forms of coordination to ensure the team can continue to function. In this phase, the interpersonal and individual demands begin to increase for the team members as well as the team leader.

PHASE 3: PURSUIT OF A COLLECTIVE GOAL

In phase 3, team members begin to understand that their individual success depends on the work of the team. A team begins to coordinate, improve, and adapt. Team functioning becomes central. However, the team becomes more fragile because team members have more to lose, both psychologically and in terms of resources. When teams disband in this phase or fail to continue, members may feel regret, disengagement, or even failure. Also, because teams have invested resources, they feel an obligation to keep the team together. Here, the team is threatened by "escalating commitment" (Staw, 1981). This means that because of the investment, teams want to continue moving toward its goal, even if it is destructive to the team members, the team, or the broader organization. The team leader helps the team by reinforcing productive beliefs such as coordinating its work, identifying ways to improve its process, and responding to potential problems that emerge in the environment.

PHASE 4: SELF-DETERMINATION

In phase 4, the team begins to sustain its own functioning by setting and pursuing its goals. Here leadership becomes less relevant; in fact, each member becomes less relevant than the larger team because the team begins to stabilize, coordinate resources, and coordinate. At this point, the team leader can begin to rest a bit easier, knowing that the team can work independently of the leader. Still, the leader plays an important role in the development of the group, although he or she does not worry about the day-to-day working of the team. Rather, the leader looks to help the team improve by gathering outside resources, buffering the team from outside distractions, and working to overcome short-term setbacks and obstacles.

PHASE 5: GROWTH

Few teams reach a level where they can innovate and work at their highest levels. But those groups who achieve phase 5 can recall the experience with fondness. Teams in this growth phase push conventional boundaries, innovate, and achieve multiple, often competing and complex, goals. The leader plays an important role in the growth phase of team functioning. Here the leader challenges the team to move beyond its current practices and processes and to engage in open conflict about its learning. In the growth phase, teams accomplish the often conflicting task of meeting individual team members' goals as well as the team's goal. At the team growth phase, individuals begin to re-evaluate their own learning, their role in the team, and their own individual goals relative to the team. Interestingly, length of time seems to play a small role in whether teams reach this stage. Recall the team led by Captain Sully; his team had been together in a time frame measured by only hours, perhaps minutes. Still they seemed to function with the highest levels of learning. Becoming a team is a starting point for team learning to occur. Next, the factors that predict team learning are discussed and then we discuss the actual process of learning on teams.

A model of team learning

We have identified eight factors that lead to effective team learning. We compared our observations with years of published research on team effectiveness and then began to conduct studies of our own to determine if these factors could be measured. We hoped to build a set of tools that could improve team learning. Dr. Melissa Knott, then a doctoral student and now on the faculty at Western New England College in Massachusetts, conducted an extensive study to further develop our eight-factor model of team learning effectiveness. Her work sought to clarify concepts and get a step closer to developing a statistically reliable and comprehensive measure for team learning effectiveness.

Working with our team of researchers, she concluded that team-learning effectiveness involves three "clusters." One cluster involves shared beliefs among team members about the nature of the task—things such as goals, roles, and confidence. A second cluster involves shared beliefs among team members about the nature of the interpersonal dynamics involved in accomplishing the task—things such as psychological safety and interpersonal understanding. The third cluster involves actions related to team learning, such as coordination, continuous improvement, and adapting. Figure 20 illustrates the relation among these team learning variables. Table 7 summarizes Dr. Knott's work and outlines the eight factors, with a definition and description of each.

BELIEFS RELATED TO TASKS

TEAM GOALS

Many believe that individuals on a team must share a common goal for a team to be successful. Theodore Mills (1967) believed that team goals don't stop at what is shared among team members—where the team is going together and what the team will accomplish. Team goals must also account for the individual goal, what individuals want to accomplish. One approach is for teams to consider both individual and team goals at the same time. Mills believed that rather than focusing on a team goal per se, teams should focus attention on shared *means,* defined as "how we are going to get there." One of the biggest problems that teams face regarding shared goals, according to Mills, is to focus too heavily on outcomes and too little on means. As a result, team goals get derailed and no one is satisfied.

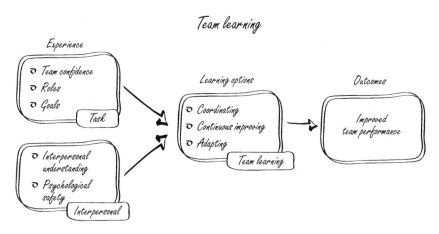

Figure 20 **Team learning**

Table 7 **Summary of team-learning beliefs and actions**

	Definition	Description
Beliefs related to tasks		
Goals	Team members' knowledge of the team and individual goals within the context of the team.	The degree to which the team members share perceptions that they have a clear and shared goal and understand individual goals in the context of the group goals.
Roles	Team members' knowledge of each other's ability.	The degree to which team members know the strengths and weaknesses of other members; know the unique skills or tasks expected of other members; and believe that tasks should be divided between members.
Team confidence	Team members' belief that the team will succeed.	The degree to which team members share the perception that they can accomplish the team's required task.
Beliefs related to relationships		
Psychological safety	Team members' belief that it is acceptable to share sensitive information.	The degree to which team members share the perception that it is acceptable to share sensitive or contrarian information. This includes admitting errors/mistakes, providing feedback, and taking challenging/controversial positions without fear of repercussions.
Interpersonal understanding	Team members' knowledge of interpersonal group dynamics.	The degree to which team members can recognize and comprehend the emotional states, preferences, or relationships of individuals in the group.
Actions related to learning		
Coordination	Team members' ability to get work done.	Team members' ability to work seamlessly together—consciously and unconsciously—to get work done, including organizing diverse roles, sharing knowledge, managing work processes, and assisting others.
Continuous improvement	Team members' ability to improve how they get work done.	Team members' ability to avoid mistakes and improve the team's performance by reviewing processes and procedures.
Adapting	Team members' ability to respond to unexpected and unusual events and still get work done.	Team members' ability to respond to unexpected and unusual demands, problems, and roadblocks—internal and external—that would prevent the team from accomplishing work.

Source: Adapted from Knott, 2009.

TEAM ROLES

Each team member brings a unique set of skills and abilities, including knowledge, different experiences (experiential diversity), and special skills. At its core, team roles describe the division of labor on the team. Team members' awareness of these team roles becomes important for learning because such awareness informs how the team will divide up the task among different team members. When deciding on roles, team leaders consider the degree to which team members know the strengths and weaknesses of other team members and the degree to which these strengths and weaknesses can be put to use in the team. Leaders build awareness of team roles by helping team members understand their unique potential and how that potential can contribute to the team's success. Team leaders help the team understand its strengths and potential weaknesses as well.

One example of the effective use of team learning roles is found with the Spanish retail group Inditex SA and its leading clothing company, Zara. Zara continues to produce higher profit margins than its competitor. This company constantly changes its fashionable clothing lines, introducing over 12,000 styles a year and refreshing its merchandise twice a week (Dutta, 2010). Zara's success comes in part from its ability to effectively use teams to produce new ideas and designs with only a short lead time. To pull this off, Zara puts together a team that regularly works together in one location. In most retailers, employees are geographically distributed and meet once a year, which requires coordinating travel schedules and extensive communication to forecast trends. Zara's team-based design approach, in contrast, combines commercial managers and designers who come together on a continuous basis and separately in their functional roles, and together as a team, establish a look, including fabric, cost, and sales price. Longer-term forecasting takes place only with the fabric. Zara retail stores, located in major cities throughout the world, play an important role in the design team as well. Trends are fed directly to the design team from store managers. Contrast this approach to that of traditional retailers, which gather fashion trend data from consumer research and feed back this information to a collection of individuals dispersed in different physical locations that come together as a team for an annual meeting. Several factors contribute to Zara's success, and its unique reliance on team roles, among other factors, has certainly been a key success factor.

TEAM CONFIDENCE

As professors and consultants, we work with hundreds of teams each year. We lead many workshops designed to improve team learning. We know from our experience, which is also supported by research, that one of the most important things we can do for a team is to build its confidence. Confident teams are teams that are better equipped to learn; they are willing to take risks and to expend effort even when they are not certain of success. To build this confidence, we often engage teams in sequential tasks. In the early phase of the team session or class, we design a task that is easy to accomplish. For example, we might send the team on a scavenger hunt to gather bits of information from around the campus or we might ask the team to build a tower out of old art scraps like paper, straws, or balloons. Anyone who has attended a team-building workshop or corporate training session will recognize these as standard team-building exercises. But the activity engages more than simply the team's sense of shared belonging. Later in the training we introduce a more complicated problem. For example, we might have the teams spend an afternoon exploring the local neighborhoods to find effective examples of leadership in the community. The team then compiles these examples and presents the information to the class, where they analyze different leadership models and their effective community role models. The second exercise presents a more complicated problem. The team presentation requires a degree of coordination, and perhaps even continuous improvement or adaptation. We deliberately make the tasks more complicated as the teams spend more time together. Our intention, and we are rarely disappointed, is to watch the teams develop a sense of accomplishment and achieve at least a minor success in the first task, then to move them on to success in later tasks that require more challenging team dynamics.

Confidence describes a general disposition a team has toward accomplishing its task. If the team is timid, confused, or generally unsure of itself, it is likely to approach learning the same way. Despite an ambiguous or changing environment, the team can build clarity and confidence around its purpose. For a team to learn at the highest levels, to thrive, it must be confident that it can achieve its goals. The team leader builds team confidence by helping it achieve small wins, encouraging the team, recognizing existing accomplishments, and creating opportunities for success.

BELIEFS RELATED TO RELATIONSHIPS

TEAM PSYCHOLOGICAL SAFETY

Whether the situation involves a commercial cockpit crew navigating a novel emergency landing, a team of designers beating the competition to stores with the latest fashion, or a group of military personnel on a routine mission, one thing becomes clear. One of the most important shared beliefs among team members is that of psychological safety. We devote Chapter 8 in this book to the importance of trust and learning-directed leadership and we discuss this concept in more depth. Here we briefly outline the importance of psychological safety for leading through learning in teams.

Dr. Amy Edmondson, a professor at Harvard University's Business School, has conducted extensive research on psychological safety and found that it is essential to effective team learning (see Edmondson, 1999; Edmondson, Bohmer, and Pisano, 2001). Her research has confirmed, using the most sophisticated behavioral science techniques available, what many group researchers have suspected for years. Fostering beliefs that lead to open conversation (that is free from retaliation for speaking up) improves team performance. Psychological safety can be measured by the degree to which team members believe it is acceptable to share sensitive or contrarian information. This includes admitting errors or mistakes, providing feedback, and taking challenging or controversial positions without fear of repercussions. This orientation goes hand in hand with interpersonal understanding.

TEAM INTERPERSONAL UNDERSTANDING

Interpersonal understanding is another shared belief related to learning. In one study, we defined and measured interpersonal understanding as the degree to which team members can recognize and comprehend the emotional states, preferences, or relationships of individuals in the group (Druskat and Kayes, 2000).

We once worked with a group of lawyers who expressed skepticism with the notion of interpersonal understanding. They suggested that it gave individuals an excuse for missing meetings or allowed them to rationalize poor work. Luckily, in the group sat an experienced attorney from the firm. He held stature and so the other, more junior attorneys looked to him for guidance in how they might react. He began with what at first appeared to be a direct challenge to the idea that improving interpersonal understanding would be accepted in his organization. "I don't care how anybody feels or if they are having a bad day," he growled. "I do know that what is going on in your life can affect your work, and that I care about. So if something is affecting your work, I want to know about it so I can either understand why you're so angry and venting it at your coworkers. I want to find a way to help you so that you can come to work more effectively," he said. With that, he made our presentation easier. There may be times when coworkers abuse the notion of interpersonal understanding, as the younger lawyers claimed; however, a better understanding of the group members and the situations that preoccupy their minds can help the team make temporary adjustments in the way it works.

ACTIONS RELATED TO TEAM LEARNING

TEAM COORDINATION: HOW WORK GETS DONE

When team members coordinate between themselves, we see team learning in action. Team learning requires team members to coordinate activities, thoughts, knowledge, and goals. Coordination, above all else, distinguishes learning as a team compared with learning individually. Without team coordination, most learning will remain locked in the heads of individuals. It is through coordination that team activities actually get done. When team coordination is at its peak, a team's experience working together is seamless. Although some coordination is conscious, other coordination is unconscious, or tacit. Tacit coordination involves an intimate understanding and coordination of roles and know-how. But just as important, tacit coordination involves knowing when to share such knowledge, when to seek help and updates from others, and when to step in and assist others.

When leading through learning, coordination of knowledge between individuals is key to effective teamwork. According to Sundstrom, De Meuse, and Futrell (1990), coordination involves developing and re-cognizing the specific knowledge of individuals, knowing when to com-municate key information, and knowing when to update the team on the progress of a project or task. One way that team leaders help facilitate team learning is by helping members identify and acknowledge the unique knowledge of team members. Then, to put this to work, team leaders help the team members synchronize this knowledge and engage in mutual adjustment. As an example, we worked in a team of four to design an educational product and its marketing plan. Two of the team members worked remotely, physically dispersed from the project. This physical separation posed a challenge, as we often worked by telephone, e-mail, or video chat. Despite the challenges, this was one of the most productive and worthwhile team experiences that we encountered. The role and task allocation was seamless; someone was always stepping in to take on tasks that we hadn't explicitly planned for. One member created a norm of checking in with everyone on the team to assess energy levels and work/life conflicts to model interpersonal understanding. Without anyone on the team explicitly asking for status updates, other members voluntarily communicated regularly about their work and how they were approaching it. Everyone on the team felt important and valuable. This stands in contrast to other teams, where we find evidence of frustration and failure with the experience.

We have found strong support of the importance of team coordination in our research over the years. In our research with undergraduate freshmen, we found that team coordination was a strong predictor of team performance. Those teams that performed best on their team project were teams that coordinated their actions, knew when to communicate key information, and reported that working together appeared to be a seamless process.

Some might challenge that what occurs in an undergraduate course doesn't directly apply to a workplace with its more pressing deadlines, fueled by internal politics and various organizational incentives. Yet we found that the same dynamics were also relevant to workplace teams. In fact, we think that these undergraduate teams are representative of behavior in a variety of contexts. Another consideration is that the particular sample we have studied consists of college freshmen, working on an ill-structured problem in a team for the very first time. In other words, these freshmen are novice team members. Evidence that novice team members improve team performance by building coordination suggests to us that coordination is a key ingredient in all teamwork (see Tsay and Kayes, 2010).

One more element of team coordination deserves attention. Effective coordination is often tacit, or unspoken. In other words, those teams that prove most effective report that they work together without thinking about it and know when to update other members of the team, even when they don't recall the specific actions. In contrast, some of the lower-performing groups reported the inability to coordinate and ranked low on survey items related to effective coordination. This suggests to us that effective teamwork is often tacit, an unspoken element that indicates effective team coordination.

CONTINUOUS IMPROVEMENT: IMPROVING HOW WORK GETS DONE

When team members learn, they work to improve on their existing performance and processes. They avoid mistakes by constantly challenging processes, reviewing procedures, and closely monitoring progress toward outcomes. Another technique related to continuous improvement is the practice of After-Action Reviews, or AARs. When teams engage in AARs, they reflect upon what occurred to better understand cause and effect relationships, identify potential errors, and find better ways to conduct teamwork in the future. One researcher observed that the Israeli Defense Force spent as much as 25 percent of operation time in AAR processes. Learning wasn't an activity that was seen as a sideline to work, but was a key part of how the team functioned (Lipshitz, Friedman, and Popper, 2006).

ADAPTING: RESPONDING TO THE UNEXPECTED

Team learning also requires adapting to unexpected roadblocks. Teams that adapt develop mechanisms to work through unusual or difficult situations. Adapting involves navigating around obstacles like unexpected and unusual demands, problems, or roadblocks. These roadblocks can arise from either internal or external demands. For example, a team may unexpectedly lose a team member or receive word that the task it faces has changed. Perhaps a client changed its requirements or a new technology won't be available as planned. An adaptation can be minor, such as when a team needs to deliver a product in a more rapid time frame than originally planned. Regardless of whether the situation calls for a dynamic or a measured response, a team's ability to adapt requires focus.

Adapting often requires a team to act in concert with the other two team-learning behaviors, coordinating and continuous improvement. Captain Chesley Sullenberger, known as "Sully," described the remarkable teamwork of his crew in response to the unexpected loss of both engines as their commercial airliner took off. The crew pulled off an unprecedented event: an emergency landing on water. This feat of team learning saved the lives of all on board the aircraft. Leaders in all walks of life can learn from the experience of how the team, led by Sully, navigated the situation. He described how, considering the time pressure to land the plane, he and his team relied on limited but "extremely time critical" communication. The limited communication was made possible by a "similar understanding of the situation" among members of his crew who were "seeing and hearing and feeling the same things" as they scanned, processed, and acted upon different sources of information (see, for example, Van Susteren, 2009). Captain Sully described team learning, the seamless process of gathering, processing, and acting upon information that is facilitated by coordinating, improving, and adapting within the team.

Team learning lies at the heart of successful leadership, not just in a near-disaster but in more common situations as well. Consider the deep yet unspoken understanding between the captain and his crew about roles and about how much and when the team would communicate. Team members constantly updated their knowledge by monitoring multiple pieces of information: What is air traffic control telling us? What are the aircraft gauges telling us? What are others doing and seeing? Finally, the team proved to be an expert at responding to unexpected demands—the loss of not one, but two engines at the same time.

LEADING LEARNING TEAMS

Like Captain Sullenberger, learning-directed leaders focus on extracting the potential of teams. Consider the case of the musical group affectionately known as the "fab four," the Beatles. Most observers agree that the Beatles

---

Strategies for leaders

Writing a team contract
The act of writing a contract together as a team allows for attention to all of the components that we have addressed. A contract is a formal agreement that the team discusses and writes, with all of the team members signing to symbolize their agreement. The terms of the contract usually include the following components:

▶ What goals they plan on accomplishing on the team (goals)
▶ Who occupies specific roles necessary for team success and when they will rotate these roles (roles)
▶ How they will build opportunities for mastery into their project; how they will know what small and large successes are (confidence)
▶ The strengths of each team member and how team members will cover for each other in an unforeseen circumstance (interpersonal understanding)
▶ Team norms or rules around what constitutes appropriate behavior; this might include defining what respectful behavior is and is not (psychological safety)
▶ How work and knowledge will be coordinated; sharing of knowledge and resources (coordination)
▶ A time frame for reevaluation of the contract, the purpose of the team, the goals of the team, the roles, etc. (continuous improvement)
▶ Specific measures on how to build change into the team and when to incorporate outside expertise and information (adapting).

was one of the most successful and innovative bands in modern music. They produced an entire list of hit songs, many of which remain popular nearly a half century after they were first produced. Yet as individual artists, many of the Beatles struggled after the band broke up. As their former manager and key producer George Martin said, "They were great individually, but they never quite reached the Olympian heights that they achieved when they were Beatles." To prove my point I often ask groups to identify more than one song that one of the Beatles (Paul McCartney or John Lennon in particular) produced that was "better" than songs they produced as Beatles. Participants offer credible and in some cases optimal songs, such as Lennon's ballad "Imagine" or McCartney's power love song "Maybe," but the main point should become clear. The Beatles consistently produced popular and long-lasting songs when they worked as a team, but as individual artists they proved less prolific. Martin believed the success of the Beatles was largely due to the working relationship between Lennon and McCartney, who were both friends and highly competitive at the same time. Each team member pushed the other to be better—a constant push to improve upon the latest contribution.

Clearly, the Beatles were something unique in history, pure music talent wrapped in a social dynamic situated in a particular social context. Yet, the lessons prove important. Learning is a social phenomenon. Whether a leader promises to define an artistic genre, like the Beatles, or simply seeks to improve output, the influence of team learning is difficult to deny. We know team members require learning beliefs and behaviors in order to engage in this social phenomenon—the process of learning. Now that we have discussed the necessary components for a team to start the learning process, we look at the specifics of this process that teams will cycle through.

Navigating the learning cycle

Learning helps teams by setting a commonly held set of shared beliefs and behaviors using appropriate levels of authority. An in-depth study of research and development teams in a large US consumer products company found that the most effective team leaders not only built a common set of shared beliefs and behaviors, but also helped the team navigate the learning cycle. We teamed up with Drs. David and Alice Kolb, both of Case Western Reserve University, to develop a model of team learning. We began with David Kolb's (1984) experiential learning cycle described in detail in Chapter 3. Kolb's model describes the individual learning cycle as a four-phase process of experience, reflection, conceptualization, and action. Building on this framework, we began to consider what this learning process might look like when it involved teams. The result was a model of team learning that tracks the organizational learning cycle but focuses on team rather than individual learning (Kayes, Kayes, and Kolb, 2005, p. 350).

STAGE 1: BUILDING SHARED PURPOSE

Stage 1, building shared purpose, corresponds to the concrete experience (feeling) mode of the experiential learning cycle. In this stage, the learning-directed leader creates the involvement and commitment of the team. The team establishes a set of shared goals while maintaining individual goals. To build team learning, a team leader might help the team articulate its purpose, as well as the individual goals. Another activity in the shared purpose stage of learning includes making the team members aware of their interdependencies, thus ensuring that the team also shares a common means to achieve the stated individual and team goals. Since this first stage will set the tone for later interactions, the team leader focuses on creating an open environment where all members can contribute and where no member dominates inappropriately.

STAGE 2: REFLECTIVE INTEGRATION

The second stage of reflective integration corresponds to the reflective observation (reflecting) mode. The learning-directed leader helps the team engage in reflection and conversation about past experiences in teams and helps to ensure all available knowledge is utilized. The team might discuss special areas of expertise, knowledge, or skills in relation to achieving its purpose. The team leader also ensures that the team discusses possible resources as well as possible setbacks that may be encountered.

STAGE 3: CRITICAL CONVERSATIONS

The critical conversations stage corresponds to the abstract concept-ualization (thinking) mode. The team leader ensures that the team thinks critically about how it works and helps the team identify new strategies and put relevant but often disparate information into a coherent plan. In this stage, the team leader ensures that the team manages information and gathers new information as appropriate.

STAGE 4: TAKING ACTION

The final stage of taking action corresponds to the active experimentation (action) mode. Here the leader establishes action plans, tests assumptions, makes decisions, and engages in further problem solving. This stage involves constantly monitoring progress toward achieving the goal and re-evaluating the goal itself.

LEADING THROUGH THE TEAM LEARNING CYCLE

A learning-directed leader can help a team navigate the learning cycle in two ways. First, the leader can ensure that the team cycles through the entire learning cycle at least once. Some teams can become stuck in a particular mode. For example, some teams tasked with a research and development goal tend to stay in the problem-solving mode and never move to action. Highly creative, these teams continue to brainstorm ideas so long that they never move to reflection. Other teams, focused on planning and design work, may linger in the development stage, never realizing the potential of their well-organized plan. In still other cases, teams may take actions that fail because they lack planning or aren't innovative. Leaders can assist their teams if they become stuck in one phase of the learning cycle.

Teams can also run into obstacles by failing to understand the importance of each stage and skipping a stage. A leader can help by determining how much time to spend in each stage of the cycle. Some teams get stuck in a phase because they lack understanding of the other stages. In an ideal situation, teams would engage in each of the four phases of the learning cycle.

Overcoming threats to team learning

The various beliefs, behaviors, and stages we have outlined so far in this chapter describe the processes that make up team learning. Team learning occurs everyday, yet many of the teams we observe fail to reach their full learning potential. An unfortunate few fail to learn much at all. Even as a team begins to learn, it must continue to overcome threats to learning.

The threats to team learning come from many sources. Psychological threats to team learning appear in the form of individual needs. The need for belonging, for example, is at the heart of the primary cause of the well-known team problem of groupthink. Groupthink occurs when critical thinking in a team fails, the team fails to consider evidence that contradicts its dominant viewpoint, and team members submit to peer pressure from other group members (Janis, 1972). Another threat to learning relates

Strategies for leaders

Over the years we have collected anecdotal stories, tips, and practices from teams that address more narrowly some of what we have discussed. Below are a composite of suggestions that teams have used to improve their focus on team learning. Teams and team leaders can use this as a guide to developing their own strategies.

▶ Building goals: Write a team charter that explains the purpose and goals of the team. The document should include the expectations and goals of individual team members.

▶ Building roles: Clarify who is responsible for each task and when it will be due to the team.

▶ Building team confidence: Take stock of team successes to date, identify experiences in past teams that were successful, and set short-term, easy-to-accomplish goals at first.

▶ Psychological safety: Take time in each meeting to gather opinions of each member, seek out alternative viewpoints, and discuss weaknesses of the current position.

▶ Interpersonal understanding: Begin each meeting with a brief "check in." For example, each person might respond to a question such as "How are you doing today?" or "What else is on your schedule?" or "Do you have anything that might be occupying your mind at this moment?"

▶ Coordination: Establish preset meeting times, even if you decide later not to meet. Decide when specific tasks are due. Exchange cell phone numbers and e-mail addresses in case there is a change of plans or later questions.

▶ Continuous improvement: Reserve no less that 5 percent of your time in meetings to discuss how things are going. Ask questions such as "What do we do well?" or "How might we improve on our work?" After particularly heated or conflict-ridden meetings, take more time and be sure to ask how the group can do things differently next time.

▶ Adapting: Establish a "turnaround time," in other words, reserve a time for reevaluation of the current goals or objectives. "Do we need to re-examine our goals?" "Do we have the right people on the project?" "Will we have access to all the resources we initially planned?" "Do we have a plan B in case we need to change our direction?"

Strategies for leaders

After Action Review (AAR) is a method to focus on learning, and we have seen these reviews take many forms. AARs can be formal processes that involve documenting a project or process in extensive detail, using page after page of data that conforms to an established protocol. AARs can also simply review past actions in an informal conversation designed to recreate events and identify potential trouble spots that might emerge in the future. In either case, the purpose of an AAR is to enhance learning from experience. The AAR process can be implemented by asking four questions (see, for example, Darling, Parry, and Moore, 2005):

1. What did we want to happen?
2. What did happen?
3. What caused the results?
4. How can we improve our actions as a team moving forward?
   a. Is there information or resources that we need?
   b. Were our goals the correct ones?
   c. What were the unintended consequences of our actions? (What happened that we did not expect to happen?)
   d. What are we going to change?

to how the group gathers and processes knowledge. One example is the common knowledge effect, in which individuals tend to share information already known among group members rather than present information that is relevant but not shared by individuals. A third threat to team learning emerges from group dynamics such as power and control. Power dynamics can derail team learning as various individuals or coalitions vie for power within the group. Power dynamics will limit the amount of psychological safety that can grow within the team. In other cases the leader becomes the focus of the team. As a result, the team fails to grow, the team leader becomes the target of the team's anxiety, and the team ultimately becomes dependent on the leader to learn (Kayes, 2004).

Conclusion

Team learning involves building shared beliefs and taking action. The development of team members involves movement from priority placed on individual agendas and goals into priority on team goals and success. Factors that will prevent learning emerge from psychological effects, failure in knowledge, and skewed power dynamics. Leaders gain expertise in modeling team learning behavior and intervening in teams that have become derailed in the learning process.

Questions for reflection

1. What experiences have I had with team learning?
2. Which components of team learning (roles, goals, adapting, etc.), on the teams that I have had experience with, have team members struggled with? Why?
3. Which components of team learning have been easy? Why?
4. What barriers to team learning have I encountered? What is my role as a leader in removing these barriers?

8 Nurturing Trust

Key ideas

▶ Trust can be nurtured at three levels in the organization: intrapersonal, interpersonal, and organizational.

▶ The intrapersonal level is about trusting yourself and having confidence in your abilities.

▶ The interpersonal level is where trust occurs between a leader and followers and trust is created as a team norm.

▶ Organizational trust is about the climate of trust at work—establishing systems and practices that promote trust and identifying systems that prevent trust.

Building trust is a basic, but often overlooked, essential of leadership. Studies show that trust is necessary for learning, it improves corporate performance, leads to increased resources, improves satisfactory working relationships, advances reputation and promotes understanding of a leader's vision. Simply put, trust is necessary for building leadership qualities. One of the most powerful reasons to nurture trust, however, is that it fosters learning. Leaders know that nurturing trust means that followers will not be afraid to speak up, challenge established norms, or surface errors. Without trust, learning fails to exist. When trust is low between leaders and followers, information gets suppressed. People hold back good ideas; insights and experiences are not shared. Nurturing an environment of trust means that all voices are heard, not just the loudest or most dominant.

A leader's story: Andrea's focus on building trust

Every time Andrea managed a project, it seemed to flourish. Peers and direct reports alike always considered Andrea an effective, efficient team leader. Andrea appeared to be headed straight to the top. As an analyst at a large manufacturing facility, she applied to become a manager in her department. Despite her prior success as a team leader, Andrea faced an impending obstacle. Jerry, a senior manager in her plant and member of her promotion review committee, remained suspicious of Andrea. In particular, he saw Andrea as too nice to be effective in the more confrontational role of manager. As a manager, Andrea would be required to enter into tough negotiations with workers on the shop floor, he thought. Jerry believed that those who received positive evaluations were probably popular and well liked. Managers shouldn't be popular, he advocated. Managers needed to make tough decisions. Popular managers showed too much concern for maintaining relationships with employees at the expense of making the hard decisions.

The promotion team considered all the internal candidates carefully before making their decision and ultimately selected Andrea over the doubts expressed by Jerry. Once promoted, Andrea continued in her trajectory of success. Not only did her projects continue to flourish, but also in her new role as manager, she often found that people in other departments and divisions requested transfers into her unit. Some often joked that whenever a job posting surfaced in Andrea's division, she had to duck and hide from the interest that surfaced. What was it about Andrea's style that made her a high performer and a sought-after manager? Why did so many people want to work on her team?

Andrea's response: "Trust, flat out. . . . I am not remarkable in other ways, but I do know how to build people's trust!" She went on to explain that she had a different style from many in her company:

> I always deliver on my promises. . . . Early in my career, I worked for a boss who continually made promises and never seemed to remember them. She was so inconsistent from day to day; I hated working at that company. It was that experience that made me swear that I would always maintain my integrity and never promise something where I couldn't follow through.

Andrea knew that empty promises kill trust.

What about Jerry's objection that popular managers don't make the tough decisions? "I know that I have to remain consistent in my actions day in and day out. I make the tough calls," Andrea noted, "but people see me as fair, so they don't hold those decisions against me personally. Rather, they try to understand the bigger picture. They know that I make decisions based on business necessity, and they think that I am fair because they trust me and my reputation and their dealings with me in the past."

Andrea gave an example:

> I had to demote someone on my team. We had adopted a new database management system and his skills were obsolete. I gave him every chance from training to a transfer and clearly spelled out the consequences if he didn't change. When I finally demoted him, he and

his team members understood the situation. They thought it was fair because I didn't fire him, but I let him continue in a lower-level job, that as it turns out was perfectly suited to his style and work capabilities. It was the process that I went through with my employees that made the difference. I have always maintained that I do not know everything and admit my mistakes and ask my people for their ideas. They can't possibly learn if they are afraid to ask questions and admit failure. My people completely supported the decision to demote him, because they saw how much I listened and remained open to being wrong.

To gain a better understanding of Andrea's reliance on trust as a key management strategy, compare her approach to that of Robert, a composite manager from our research. Robert had the reputation for being inconsistent. His employees never knew what to expect with him: one day he was in a good mood and pleasant to be around, and the next day he would turn on his staff and scold them for no apparent reason. Sometimes, he would issue a decision based solely on the company's policy (he could even quote long sections from the handbook and was known to do so!), and the next day, he would make a decision that went against the very policy he quoted the day before.

The biggest problem, according to his employees, was that Robert's decisions appeared to be arbitrary. In fact, Robert's decisions seemed so arbitrary that his staff had little trust in him. The difference between Andrea and Robert became clear when we talked to his staff about a time he demoted one of his employees. Robert faced a much different reaction from his employees than Andrea did when she demoted the software engineer in her department. His employees didn't understand his decision and did not think that he had their best interest at heart and they certainly would not voice these concerns directly to their boss. The reaction of Robert's staff is quite common; trust seems to be lacking in many workplaces.

The challenges of building trust

Given the importance of trust, there is still a surprising lack of trust reported in organizations. A 2001 Gallup poll reported that only 41 percent of Americans said most people could be trusted. Nearly 80 percent polled did not trust top executives. A 2005 Gallup poll found that only 16 percent of Americans ranked honesty and ethical standards of business executives as high or very high. These studies imply that leaders looking to build trust face a difficult task.

Trust includes many different things. Leaders who nurture trust can be relied on, and they promote learning through an open and accepting environment. As a result, individuals feel they can bring up tough issues, reflect on solutions while placing personal agendas aside, and openly discuss weaknesses of the team, and surface problems or errors that may arise.

One leader we know begins his weekly meetings by asking his team to talk about mistakes they made during the past week and how they can improve. The sessions prove more than a gripe session. All team members take seriously the notion that they will be expected to openly identify their weakness. More importantly, team members know they will be responsible for helping other team members overcome their mistakes and problems. The leader is consistent with what Alan Fox (1974), a noted British industrial sociologist, has said about trust and leadership. Fox explained trust from a microsociological perspective. First, trust is reciprocal in nature. If one team member trusts another, then other members are more likely to trust each other. On the other hand, if team members mistrust each other, then in turn others will be mistrustful. Second, trust does not know neutrality—there is only trust or distrust in the workplace.

Unfortunately, in our work, we have seen many more examples of distrust than trust. One organization we worked for turned out to be particularly challenging in the area of trust building. We were asked to visit a highly successful team in a major US telecommunications firm. The team had proven their effectiveness time and again. In fact, the team remained one of the company's top-performing operational teams. Yet the team members remained dissatisfied with their work. They asked us to come in and help them improve. After some time with the team, including application of some of the team diagnostic tools found in this book, we began to realize that the team had low trust. Even more difficult for our work as consultants, we realized the team harbored their lack of trust toward the team leader, the person who hired us! Many on the team believed that the team leader bullied other members; she had a "what I say goes" attitude that stifled the team's ability to bring up the tough issues necessary to take their performance to another level. In the end, the team continued to stagnate because they mistrusted their team leader. Only after the team leader left and the team itself split apart did members of the team begin to even consider trusting again.

Types of trust

Despite the difficulty of building trust, many leaders succeed in nurturing trust. An easy way to foster trust in your leadership involves thinking about

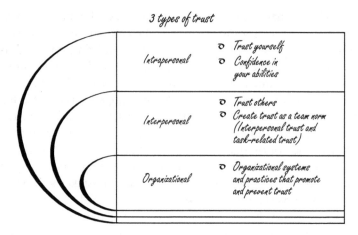

Figure 21 **Types of trust**

trust as occurring in three different areas: intrapersonal, interpersonal, and organizational. Figure 21 shows the three types of trust in the workplace.

INTRAPERSONAL

Trusting starts with trusting yourself, which is called *intrapersonal trust.* This involves trusting your capabilities and your followers' capabilities, your decisions and your followers' decisions, and your potential impact on those around you. Dr. Jack Gibb, a psychologist who devoted his career to understanding trust in organizations, thought that the starting point for trust was self-trust and called this *realizing.* Realizing is being all that you can be. It involves connecting with people and building relationships with them over time. Realizing, which is built on the humanistic tradition that recognizes self-understanding and change, is the first step of the trust process, because self-understanding is the building block of all good trusting relationships. Self-understanding is dependent on the richness of the environment in which you work. That is, it is hard to work in an environment that is based on mistrust and fear and still be all that you can be and connect and develop meaningful relationships based on trust. In previous chapters we have discussed the importance of reflection in the learning process. Through reflection, leaders learn to better understand and trust themselves.

Intrapersonal trust also improves confidence. It takes a lot of confidence to rely on others to accomplish work, to make decisions, and to share the spotlight. Allowing others to do these things can feel threatening. Recall the discussions on efficacy in the section on resilience. Building efficacy was about building confidence and letting go of anxieties and fears. The process of efficacy building helps to lay the foundation for other forms of trust, such as interpersonal trust.

INTERPERSONAL

Interpersonal trust is an exchange of trust between you and your followers: you trust someone and he or she trusts you. You can create trust at the interpersonal level by being honest about your goals, your intentions, and your faults and failures as well as your strengths. It also involves being credible and consistent in how you are perceived by your followers. In order to better understand trust, it is useful to look at the "bases of trust." Gabarro (1978) undertook a three-year groundbreaking study designed to determine the process by which relationships are established between new company presidents and their subordinates. The research found that trust in interpersonal relationships is formed based on perceptions of another's character, competence, and judgment. He outlined three elements of trust:

Character:
- Trust in the other's integrity
- Trust in the other's motives and intentions
- Trust in the other's consistency of behavior
- Trust in the other's openness and discreetness

Competence:
- Trust in the other's functional or specific competence
- Trust in the other's interpersonal competence
- Trust in the other's general business sense

Judgment:
- Trust in the other's ability to make good judgments in work and behavior
(Gabarro, 1978, p. 295).

According to Marshall Sashkin, an expert on leadership and trust and author of *Visionary Leadership* and *Leadership that Matters*, credibility and consistency are outcomes based on the perception of your character, competence, and judgment. But building credibility and consistency takes time. *Credibility* is a measurement of whether you, as a leader, actually do what you say you are going to do. Credibility comes from four activities:

1. Accurately reporting your performance and accomplishments
2. Doing what you previously stated you would do

3. Fulfilling promises that you previously made
4. Accurately stating results or outcomes

Sashkin's four dimensions of credibility of leaders require that you model the right behavior for others by doing what you say you will do (Sashkin and Sashkin, 2003).

The second dimension is *consistency*. For followers to perceive you as a consistent leader, you must exhibit the same set of behaviors over time, given the same situation. Another way to discuss consistency is to say that it fosters predictability of your behavior. You will display consistency in your leadership behavior when you display the same sort of qualities and behaviors when you interact with different people or display the same type of qualities and behaviors when you interact with the same person over time in the same manner. If you are patient with one employee who is slow to learn and are visibly impatient and sarcastic with another employee who is slow to learn, you will be viewed as inconsistent and difficult to form a trusting relationship with.

Developing trust as a team norm

Trust can be viewed as a team norm and even as a reputation attached to team membership. Interdepending, a type of team norm, is when individuals learn how to relate as a team. This involves people putting aside their self-interests and putting the needs of the team and the organization first. It involves relying on your followers and not trying to accomplish everything yourself.

Gibb introduced a series of common trust issues in interdepending on new teams and a method for diagnosing them that leaders have found useful over the years. A new team is a team that has just formed, has added or lost a member, or has not met for a while. Trust is the thermometer that gauges the health of a group. He argued that for teams to work through their issues related to trust, they would have to move through issues hierarchically, resolving one before moving on to the next issue. Table 8 depicts each area of trust for a team and what these areas look like when they are resolved. So, if a team had issues in control, it was because they had not adequately worked through aims. A team may have an issue with power struggles and carrying out its work effectively, and it may be that the group has not adequately agreed on the purpose of the team and what work they needed to accomplish together.

In addition to establishing trust as a stated or unstated rule of team behavior, some members benefit from their reputation as being part of

Table 8 **Team trust concerns**

Team concern	How this concern is manifested	Resolved
Acceptance (*who is included in the team, belonging*)	Fear, distrust	Acceptance, trust
Information (*data necessary to complete tasks*)	Hidden feelings, difficulty in making decisions, caution, forced politeness	Sharing, development of decision-making techniques
Aims (*purpose of the team*)	Competition, apathy	Creative work
Control (*how work is distributed and who is in charge*)	Dependency, counter-dependency, power struggles	Role distribution based on individual strengths

Source: Adapted from Gibb, 1964.

a specific team. Williams (2001) noticed that some employees have the reputation of being trustworthy based only on who they are associated with, and she decided to study this dynamic more systematically. Findings in this study indicate that beliefs about a group influence the perceived trustworthiness of an individual who belongs to that group. In other words, if people label a group as trustworthy, then they will label people in the group as trustworthy. If you have an employee who was a former Eagle Scout and volunteers with the scouting organization on the weekends, you might be more inclined to trust him as a member of your work group because you trust the Boy Scouts as a group. Trust is a necessary part of healthy group life in the workplace and is essential for group functioning and learning. Functioning and learning effectively can also be tied to the overall climate in the workplace.

Trust as part of the workplace climate

The organizational level of trust is about the general climate of trust in an organization and those systems in the organization that promote or detract from the climate of trust. At the macro level of trust, the climate in an organization is related to the other levels of trust we discussed—intrapersonal and interpersonal as well as other factors. It is leaders who construct the climate of trust in organizations. Leaders determine what values and patterns of behavior are emphasized, modeled, and rewarded. The climate of trust in an organization is built through a process that leaders can learn to replicate.

THE CLIMATE OF TRUST AMONG CORRECTIONAL OFFICERS

One of the authors, Anna, conducted a study on climates of trust with correctional officers in a series of prisons in the southeastern United States. The prisons in her study ranged from maximum to minimum security and all housed male offenders. Among the 400+ officers involved in her study, about half were women and half were men. For the purposes of the study, trust was defined for the officers as the climate established by the top executives in the organization, the warden and his immediate management team. The correctional officers were viewed as frontline supervisors in this type of environment, responsible for supervision of inmates and facilities. Anna hypothesized that there would be a high climate of trust between top management and frontline supervisors (Kayes, A. B., 2004). Correctional institutions have been compared to military units, and many military units only function well with high levels of trust, so this seemed like a reasonable set of hypotheses. Surprisingly, the findings showed low levels of trust in all of the prisons compared with other types of organizations using the same survey methodology. There were no differences in climates of trust by level of security; maximum-security prisons had trust that was just as low as in minimum-security prisons.

One possible explanation for these results is the presence of *fear*. Gibb (1978) explained that in an environment containing fear, punishment and an autocratic structure are evident. When people are in the stage of fear, they do not trust anyone, and punishment is one of the primary means in which people interact. Punishment can be conceptualized as occurring upward between subordinate and superior and is evidenced through blame and hostility. If punishment is the primary means of interpersonal interactions, the overall climate of an organization will not nurture trust. Research shows that environments low in trust will produce autocratic mechanisms, evidenced by suppression of emotions, hierarchy of power and control, and the feeling of powerlessness by employees. This study of prisons shows us that trust does not automatically occur in organizations, that it must be built carefully by leaders and can just as easily be destroyed and replaced by another type of culture based on fear, powerlessness, and blame. The next organization shows us a different picture of organizational climate.

THE CLIMATE OF TRUST AND A MILITARY TEAM IN THE IRAQI WAR

One organization that bears mention relative to trust is the US Army during combat in Iraq. Now, this is a military example, and some leaders in private organizations might wonder how leadership during military combat is relevant or applicable to other types of organizations. Organizations that include law enforcement, medical teams, and firefighting are easy parallels, but lessons from combat leaders are more broadly applicable for several reasons. First, the essence of leadership emerges during periods of extreme stress. This stress is present in most organizations. As organizations are being scrutinized and under intense, sometimes chaotic, pressures to perform and meet higher and higher standards with limited resources, so too were military leaders during the Iraq war. Second, nurturing trust is one of the leadership practices that can easily dissolve during periods of stress if it is not practiced effectively. Finding an example of an organization that maintained high levels of leader and subordinate trust during periods of stress was not an easy feat. Finally, the stakes of leader actions and the high degree of leader accountability in a combat example are an interesting extreme to gauge the stakes of leader actions and leader responsibility in noncombat contexts. Leaders in nonmilitary organizations wrestle with issues of stress, complexity, uncertainty, accountability, and perseverance while trying to build, repair, and maintain trust in their organizations. Leaders in the military struggle with these same issues, but they are trusting people with their lives, not simply their livelihoods. When Dr. Allen conducted a study of military leaders during the Iraqi war, he was interested in how they learned and how they built a climate of learning for others (Allen, 2006).

Dr. Allen noticed how leaders involved in combat in places such as Iraq and Afghanistan constantly had to build and maintain trust, as well as learn from experience quickly. But building leadership among your own troops, those in your command, proved the easy part. The most effective military leaders deepened and developed trust with their followers *and* with the larger community. Trust relied on keeping everyone in the loop on agendas and plans and being consistent and credible with the crafting of communication. As one leader explained:

> I have to work overtime at letting my soldiers know what's going on. Soldiers will do anything, but they have to know what's going on. So, about twice a month, I get together and give them an update on what's going on and what we are accomplishing. . . . It's easy to forget the importance of getting that information out to the lowest level. The leaders will know but the soldiers won't.
>
> (p. 76)

Another leader Dr. Allen interviewed reflected on the challenge of taking over a unit. This leader wanted his troops to be more aware of their impact on the Iraqi community where they patrolled. He emphasized the importance of being credible and communicating in building relationships based on trust with the community. The leader recalled his initial concerns when taking over the new command.

> My assessment of the company when I took over was that they were operating without much regard for the populace . . . not a lot of insight into long term what they were going to accomplish and what the end state would be and how they were going to get there. . . . You have to balance aggressive combat operations with humanity and compassion toward the locals. And that applies to how we conduct ourselves on and off the streets. . . . There's a balance to mitigating the risks and protecting the civilians. And part of it is just communicating with civilians verbally and visually.
>
> (p. 78)

Yet, despite his intentions, the commander expressed how difficult it was to build trust with a community where fear ran rampant. He noted that soldiers were suspicious of civilians, civilians were suspicious of soldiers, and the civilians were even suspicious of one another. He recounted an example where a military officer engaged with civilians. He agreed to sit down and have tea with them, which he thought was a gesture of trust.

Another leader Dr. Allen interviewed, a new leader, emphasized honesty in his encounters with his staff. This new commander described a particularly difficult situation where he instituted a new policy that was unpopular. The new policy resulted in an accident, and the accident set off an official investigation:

> During the investigation I was honest: "Here are the facts as I know them." And the next thing I know I felt like I was the guy under fire—it was a hostile environment. . . . [The investigator] asked me my thought process on why I did so, and he said, "I see what you were thinking, but I disagree with you." . . . The leaders in my company later told me they thought I did the right thing. . . . I got to where I was spending a lot more time talking to my soldiers trying to get to know them. I've learned things about my guys that I probably would have never learned if [the accident] hadn't happened.
>
> (p. 87)

These leaders recounted many hard lessons learned in their struggle to be effective with their followers and in the community. None of the leaders interviewed said that trust was easy to build. Rather, each leader worked at it and struggled with it. Nurturing trust took time. These leaders all recounted the tremendous value of learning in building the process of trust and applying these hard experiences to develop their team and accomplish their mission.

The military teams building a climate of trust were similar to other teams that we reviewed. Remember the discussion in Chapter 7 on team learning around psychological safety? Studies of psychological safety showed that leaders in airplane cockpit crews that fostered an environment of trust had lower error rates and could respond to unexpected problems more completely (Edmondson, 1999). Leaders who were consistent and credible, as well as open to the opinions of others in the crew, were more likely to identify problems, allow them to surface, and respond appropriately. In contrast, among cockpit crews with low trust, captains tended to ignore important information and appeared disinterested in the views, opinions, or perceptions of others in the cockpit.

Even as a passenger, you can identify little bits of openness and nurturing of trust. The next time you fly on a commercial airliner, listen to the captain's greeting to the passengers. Does she sound open, interested, and genuinely excited to be speaking to you? Or does she seem like communicating the message over the intercom is a burden? You might begin to determine if the cockpit has low or high levels of trust. Trust is important for learning because it responds to a basic psychological need, freedom from fear.

Barriers to trust

Fear is the enemy of trust in organizations. Fear causes people to mask information, hide agendas, distort the truth, point fingers, blame others, and avoid talking about important issues that might lead to learning and improving. In the study of prisons, the author surmised that this was why the overall climate of trust was so low (Kayes, A. B., 2004). Leaders who nurture trust help bring to the surface issues that block learning. According to Peter Senge, author of *The Learning Organization*, in climates of fear, leaders cannot build the trust that they need to repair and focus on these important issues (Senge, 1990).

Chris Argyris (1991) described another reason trust is so important for learning. Often, he argued, leaders operate under the wrong set of assumptions. In essence, a leader can be completely unaware that her followers are suspicious of her and afraid to tell her the truth about problems. The followers then try to figure out what is really going on. Often the followers attribute erroneous causes to leadership behavior. For example, the follower might think the leader disapproves of his behavior or is against his idea. But this guesswork about what the leader is actually thinking just makes the problem worse. Leaders who are open and honest set the tone for better, more trusting relationships. The payoff, according to Argyris, is greater learning (p. 107) as discussed in Chapter 2.

Leaders have a responsibility to examine systems that might be supporting a culture of fear. In addition to surfacing assumptions that people have, a broader scan of the organization and identification of factors contributing to a culture of blame and finger-pointing are extremely valuable in eliminating fear. Trust moves in when fear moves out. Finally, as managers learn how to survey the organization and identify problem areas, they should also understand how the organization fits into the broader environment and how that relationship can trigger fear.

Driving out fear and nurturing trust prove tricky for leaders. Nurturing trust comes only after hard work from the leader and is an ongoing process; a leader has to always engage in this hard work. Fear, in contrast, comes from a variety of sources. Fear stems from a variety of organizational mechanisms such as individual background and past experiences, established systems within the organization, HR practices, and even environmental issues such as crises or critical incidents. We explore each of these in more depth.

INDIVIDUAL BARRIERS

To start with, people need to learn how to reason productively and question the reasoning of others. Faulty reasoning can often lead people to assume that there are punishments associated with being honest or forthright and with revealing agendas and issues at work. Faulty reasoning can also lead to pointing fingers at either the leader or the organization (Kets de Vries and Miller, 1984; Janis, 1972).

A government contracting group that we worked with illustrates the problem. At one of their meetings, a team member came prepared with data to support why their project had fallen behind schedule. He blamed the finance officer and said that it was his fault they were behind schedule because they were not getting the financial resources they needed in time to complete the staffing of their team. Accusations began to fly, members blamed various leaders in the organization, and the meeting started to deteriorate into a perfect example of unproductive reasoning. We provided a set of tools for this team that allowed them to ask questions and gather data to facilitate more productive conversation. As it turned out, there was a very simple explanation for the delay in resource allocation.

The team had never submitted the paperwork requesting the additional staff member. They jumped to conclusions and assumed the finance officer was trying to sabotage their success. After this came out in discussions, the team later enjoyed the humor in the situation. The energy spent blaming the finance officer and being angry at missing deadlines was wasted. The team could have been learning how to navigate the difficult terrain of government contracts. The problem with false assumptions is that they lead to faulty decision-making and inhibit trust and learning. These false assumptions also contribute to a culture of "groupthink" that becomes difficult to change (Janis, 1972) as people hold on to their faulty assumptions and pressure others to believe them as well.

SYSTEMATIC BARRIERS

Second, if reasoning is not the issue, other system-wide mechanisms may be preventing employee trust. HR practices that do not address the needs of employees (Costigan et al., 2004)—or, more specifically, the system of rewards and punishments—might be causing an environment of fear. If rewards and punishments are not aligned with what the organization or the manager hopes for, then one result is a loss of trust and counterproductive behavior (see, for example, Kets de Vries and Miller, 1984; Kerr, 1995).

Paul was the perfect example of the "go to" person in his law firm. He handled records administration and was a very dependable employee. He always handled the special projects, last-minute work assignments, and

---

Strategies for leaders: Testing attributions and assumptions against data

The way to easily check whether an error in reasoning exists is to dissect the process of reasoning. These five steps can be used for other people's reasoning and *your* reasoning as well.

1. Identify the conclusions someone is making.
2. Seek out the data that lead to the conclusion.
3. Ask for the reasoning or logic trail that connects the data with the conclusion.
4. Identify a possible belief or assumption.
5. Test what you identified with the person.

other tasks and duties that needed to be done because he would find a way to complete them. Paul complained that his team members had learned that if they did not want to do a particularly dull or difficult task, they would slow down. Promptly, the task would be handed off to Paul, because he was the most efficient. From a manager's perspective, this seemed like the right thing to do: assign work to someone who would get it done. Paul felt that this was a punishment, because he always ended up with the most undesirable work projects. Meanwhile, his team members had less work and more interesting work, plus the same compensation. In effect, Paul's good behavior was punished.

ENVIRONMENTAL BARRIERS

A climate of fear could also be related to a recent crisis at work or a critical incident (see, for example, Coombs, 2006, 2007). A crisis is a "condition of instability leading to a change where people experience fear of the unknown," such as the following:

▶ A dramatic restructuring
▶ An upheaval in management
▶ A financial crisis, a shortage of resources (people or other)

A critical incident, on the other hand, is "an isolated incident that people make meaning out of and attribute to the climate of fear," such as the following:

▶ The firing of a visible and well-liked employee
▶ The atypical berating of an employee by a manager who is going through a personal difficulty
▶ The demotion of someone who becomes a symbol for everyone

There are many suggestions for managing crises and critical incidents. Leaders should select the tools available for their use. For crises, leaders should communicate the impending changes and how they will affect everyone involved. This approach serves to minimize the fear of the unknown caused by the crisis. If there is a critical incident, leaders should determine how they can help people move past an isolated incident and return to normal. This may involve something as small as providing positive feedback and open communication or something as significant as investing in the company's employee assistance program or confidential counseling referral service. The point is to determine the cause of the critical incident, how people have interpreted it, and how the leaders

Strategies for leaders: Analyzing the reward system

Analyze the outcomes and intentions of the system of rewards and consequences and change those that are not effective. Table 9 presents some examples of how you might analyze the outcomes and intentions of consequences present in your organization. If there is no alignment between consequences and hopes, there may be an environment of fear. These questions, while useful for analysis of your current environment, are also useful to *predict* what might happen when designing a new system or trying to change consequences in your organization.

Table 9 **Analyzing the reward system**

Reward or consequence	What organization/ manager hopes for	What is actually being rewarded or punished	Is this effective?	Why?
More work projects for people who are dependable	Accomplish work goals as easily and as effectively as possible	*Rewarding* those who are not as committed or skilled at accomplishing work tasks and *punishing* those who are motivated and skilled	Not in the long term	People are afraid to take initiative because it means they will be punished with more work
Making an example out of someone	Pressure others to conform a certain way; teach the right way	Rewarding those who cover their mistakes and who successfully pin the blame on someone else	Not in the long term	People are afraid to own up to mistakes because they may be embarrassed in front of their peers; this contributes to blame and finger-pointing

can encourage them to put it behind them. Leaders might offset an unfortunate situation by taking a risk and doing something out of the normal course of business. When they are negative, critical incidents can undermine the culture of trust in an organization. Critical incidents that are positive are a lesson for everyone on the leader's ability to take risks and trust someone.

Conclusion

Leaders, in particular, have an advantage when they can create and sustain relationships based on self-trust, trust in others, and an organizational climate of trust, fixing the climate when trust breaks down. Diagnosing common errors and incidents to build on a climate of trust takes time and perseverance. The payoff in the end is a culture where the leader is seen as honest and her people will follow her—not because they have to, but because she engages their minds, follows through on her promises, and offers them an opportunity to make mistakes and to learn and grow.

Questions for reflection

1. How can you improve the work environment to make sure that people feel it is safe to express their differences?
2. How can you improve communication to make sure that your people know your agendas and intentions?
3. How do the reward and consequence systems in your organization support or detract from trust?
4. How can you develop others to build trust in their relationships, their organization, and their community?

Conclusion

Throughout this book we have encouraged leaders to engage in the learning process as they develop self and others in their organizations. The six practices provide areas to focus such learning. By engaging in the process of learning, leaders cultivate forces that improve individual and organizational performance. These practices provide a baseline. The assumptions, theory, research, and practice on which these six practices were built serve only as a starting point. But beware. In many organizations, learning takes a back seat to other organizational practices. Many organizations measure and reward performance and achievement at the expense of learning and learning-directed leadership. Nonetheless, leadership is often required to make learning an explicit practice in organizations. In many cases, effective learning requires leaders to communicate its value to competing and flourishing in today's frenetic, fast-paced, and complex environment.

Learning is seldom a simple process. Recall David Kolb's (1984) principles for learning from experience. We presented the principles in more detail in Chapter 3. Here is a restating of his principles in the context of learning-directed leadership.

▶ Learning is a process, not an outcome, and takes deliberate practice and motivation.

▶ Leaders' individual experience and the experience of others is the basis for learning. Real learning requires surrounding oneself with others who desire to learn. Learning is contagious.

▶ Learning results from a resolution of competing ways of processing and acting on information. There is not one "right" style of learning but many approaches. Learning doesn't just happen in a classroom but can occur in almost any situation.

▶ Learning is holistic and expansive, which is not always in line with short-term, results-driven organizational goals.

▶ Learning occurs when leaders engage with their environment. Leadership requires higher-order learning in order to respond to multiple, complex, and novel demands of leadership.

▶ Learning creates new ideas and knowledge. Innovation and risk are involved in learning. Leaders' confidence in their ability to learn, in adaptive practices in their organizations, and trust of themselves and others are necessary to create knowledge.

Engaging in reflective practice

As part of the learning process, we have encouraged leaders to become more reflective, to seek higher-level learning opportunities, to assess their emotional intelligence competencies, to build efficacy, and to trust—and to foster these practices in others. Developing each of these practices takes time. Reflection involves looking back at past experiences, events, or situations with the intent of improving understanding. Again, the challenges of contemporary leadership make finding time for reflection difficult. Building reflection into leadership practice requires focus in both the short and long term. In the Introduction, we described the learning-directed leadership cycle in five stages. An additional consideration is cycle time. How fast does a leader work through each cycle? We suggest that, for planning purposes, a leader consider four distinct "zones" or learning time frames (Griffiths and Tann, 1991). Leaders can consider learning in each zone.

▶ Zone 1 learning involves learning that has long-term consequences, as measured in years, decades, or even generations. Zone 1 learning focuses on development and long-term change and lifecycle adaptation.
▶ Zone 2 learning focuses on a time frame of 1–3 years. While this is relatively short term, most organizations focus on this time frame.
▶ Zone 3 learning concentrates on a year or less.
▶ Zone 4 learning centers attention on learning that has immediate impact measured in minutes, seconds, or hours. This is where crisis management occurs.

Leaders need to consider the time frame of learning and develop learning plans that address learning in each zone.

Development of others

Learning involves the leader, the led, and the context or environment in which this interaction takes place. *The Learning Advantage* emphasizes the importance of developing the "led" in the leader equation as well as the leader. Development is the work of leaders, and sharing mastery of knowledge creation is important work. A number of methods encourage learning in others. Here are a few methods.

ACTION LEARNING

In Chapter 2, we introduced the theoretical basis of *The Learning Advantage*, including action learning, which is learning in direct service of solving organizational problems. This action-learning methodology encourages learning as people work together on an unfamiliar problem and rely on questioning and supporting each other's learning. Many resources are designed narrowly around action-learning methods and how to design, facilitate, and troubleshoot action-learning teams (see, for example, Marquardt, 1999; Raelin, 2003).

In our experience of working with leaders, we have found that this is a practical and highly useful mechanism to encourage learning in others, even others who are skeptical about the pragmatic value of learning. One large international bank we worked with during their merger instituted action-learning teams that focused on finding solutions to talent management problems and motivation. The process of action learning encouraged team members to develop learning competencies while solving important organizational problems. As a result, actions of these teams led to improvements in key organizational metrics, such as turnover and satisfaction, but even more importantly, team members built skills in leadership.

COACHING

Coaching in all its forms, peer-to-peer, executive, career, provides a valuable method for facilitating learning in others. Many formal learning programs in the workplace cajole leaders into signing up to be a mentor, procuring a peer coach, or accepting an executive coaching arrangement. The quality of these learning interventions varies as much on the basis of the qualifications, integrity, and personal characteristics of the coach as it does with the motivation of the person being coached. When the process is done right, it is powerful, but when the process is missing a key ingredient, it can be a disaster. Even given the trickiness of executing coaching in an ethical and impactful manner, it remains a solid method for learning development.

Coaching is now a formal benefit in many graduate programs targeting current and future leaders. At The George Washington University School of Business, executive MBA students learn rigorous academic content and are expected to grow their knowledge base over the years of the program. Increased knowledge bases alone, however, do not translate into the best future leaders. A program was integrated into the management curriculum to assign students a skilled coach who would work with them on their personal development, ensuring that if the students were willing, they would gain valuable personal insights, increased awareness of relationship management, and learning competencies that would give them an edge over graduates from more traditional MBA programs. That learning is holistic and integrated. It reminds students and their coaches to connect work experiences, personal experiences, and the curriculum into a meaningful package. The mutual learning experiences that we have had with coaching others have encouraged us to mention this as a method for learning development.

FEEDBACK AND OTHER LEARNING REWARDS

Most people are familiar with the adage that the behavior that you reward is the behavior that continues. This is based on well-developed research that ties behavior to consequences. There is some criticism of attaching praise and rewards to learning, but well-thought-out feedback is helpful. Praising employees each time they engage in a learning activity might be viewed as insincere, manipulative, or even patronizing. But, a useful way to encourage others to embrace learning is to praise well. Research on adult learning in the workplace (see, for example, Keller, 1992) gives us insight as to what effective praise and reward might be:

1. Provide learning-directed encouragement with sincerity, spontaneity, and other signs of credibility. Many adults in executive education workshops comment that sincerity is the most important of these criteria.
2. Link learning to other pragmatic considerations. People want to feel that learning is useful. Providing feedback that connects individuals' learning behaviors with a pragmatic outcome is helpful. For instance, after noticing that an employee is taking the initiative to read a leadership book, a leader can provide feedback on how developing knowledge around leadership is an effective way to learn the challenges associated with the next level of position in the organization.
3. Link success at learning to the person's own achievement or capabilities. Remember our discussions on efficacy and control in Chapter 5? A leader might provide praise and make the connections between new learning skills and the person's motivation to learn, competence, or other positive personal attribute. This boosts efficacy and the perception of control. For example, when noticing that someone has improved her ability to

engage in critical thinking, a leader can provide praise saying that he knew that she could do it, because she has always demonstrated qualities like perseverance or intelligence.

The use of positive feedback, along with the other six practices described in this book provide leaders with concrete actions to guide their leadership, hone their learning skills, and build learning capacity in self and others. As they implement an approach to leadership that is tied to development of themselves, their followers, and their organization, we believe that they will gain the advantage in the ever-changing and uncertain workplaces.

References

Ackermann, R. and DeRubeis, R. J. (1991). Is depressive realism real? *Clinical Psychology Review, 11*, 565–584.

Allen, N. L. (2006). Leader development in dynamic and hazardous environments: Company commander learning in combat. Unpublished PhD dissertation, The George Washington University, Washington, DC.

Allen, N. and Kayes, D. C. (2010). Leader development in dynamic and hazardous environments: Company commanders in combat. In A. McKee and M. Eraut (Eds), *Professional Learning Over the Lifespan: Innovation and Change*. New York, NY: Springer.

American Management Association (2007). *How to Build a High Performance Organization*. New York, NY: Author. Retrieved from http://www.gsu.edu/images/HR/HRI-high-performance07.pdf

American Psychological Association (n.d.). *The Road to Resilience* [brochure]. Washington, DC: Author. Retrieved from http://www.apa.org/helpcenter/road-resilience.aspx

Argyris, C. (1980). *Inner Contradictions of Rigorous Research*. New York: Academic Press.

Argyris, C. (1991). Teaching smart people how to learn. *Harvard Business Review, 69*(3), 99–109.

Argyris, C. and Schon, D. (1978). *Organizational Learning: A Theory of Action Perspective*. Reading MA: Addison-Wesley.

Bailey, J. and Kayes, D. C. (2005). Learning, individual. In N. Nicholson, P. G. Audia, and M. M. Pillutla (Eds), *The Blackwell Encyclopedia of Management* (2nd edn, vol. XI, pp. 213–215). London, UK: Blackwell.

Balcetis, E. (2008). Where the motivation resides and the self-deception hides: How motivated cognition accomplishes self-deception. *Social and Personality Psychology Compass, 2*, 361–381.

Bandura, A. (1997). *Self-Efficacy: The Exercise of Control*. New York, NY: W. H. Freeman & Co.

Berenholtz, S. M., Pronovost, P. J., Lipsett, P. A., Hobson, D., Earsing, K., Farley, J. E., Milanovich, S., Garrett-Mayer, E., Winters, B. D., Rubin, H. R., Dorman, T., and Perl, T. M. (2004). Eliminating catheter-related bloodstream infections in the intensive care unit. *Critical Care Medicine, 32*, 2014–2020.

Bloom, B. S. (1956). *Taxonomy of Educational Objectives, the Classification of Educational Goals—Handbook I: Cognitive Domain*. New York: McKay.

Boje, D.M. (2001). *Narrative Methods for Organizational and Communication Research*. London: Sage.

Boje, D. M. and Dennehy, R. E (1993). *Managing in the Postmodern World: America's Revolution against Exploitation.* Dubuque, IA: Kendall/Hunt.

Boyatzis, R. E. (2006). Using tipping points of emotional intelligence and cognitive competencies to predict financial performance of leaders. *Psicothema, 18,* 124–131.

Boyatzis, R. (2009). Competencies as a behavioral approach to emotional intelligence. *Journal of Management Development, 28,* 749–70.

Cameron, K., Dutton, J. E., and Quinn, R. E. (2003). *Positive Organizational Scholarship.* San Francisco, CA: Berrett-Koehler Publishers.

Cannon, M. and Edmundson, A. (2005). Failing to learn and learning to fail (intelligently): How great organizations put failure to work to innovate and improve. *Long Range Planning, 38,* 299–319.

Chi-Sum, W., Ping-Man, W., and Peng, K. (2010). Effect of middle-level leader and teacher emotional intelligence on school teachers' job satisfaction: The case of Hong Kong. *Educational Management Administration & Leadership, 38,* 59–70. doi:10.1177/1741143209351831.

Clarke, N. (2010). Emotional intelligence and its relationship to transformational leadership and key project manager competencies. *Project Management Journal, 41,* 5–20. doi:10.1002/pmj.20162

Coombs, W. T. (2006). *Code Red in the Boardroom: Crisis Management as Organizational DNA.* Westport, CT: Praeger.

Coombs, W. T. (2007). *Ongoing Crisis Communication: Planning, Managing, and Responding* (2nd edn). Thousand Oaks, CA: Sage.

Costigan, R., Insinga, R., Kranas, G., Kureshov, V., and Ilter, S. (2004). Predictors of employee trust of their CEO: A three-country study. *Journal of Managerial Issues, 16,* 197–216.

Coutu, D. (2002a, March). An interview with Edgar Schein. The anxiety of learning: The darker side of organizational learning. *Harvard Business Review, 80*(3), pp. 100–106.

Coutu, D. (2002b). How resilience works. *Harvard Business Review, 80*(5), 46–55.

Dalton, G. W. and Thompson, P. H. (1993). *Novations: Strategies for Career Management.* Novations Group.

Darling, M., Parry, C., and Moore, J. (2005). Learning in the thick of it. *Harvard Business Review,* July/August, 84–92.

Dehler, G. E., Welsh, M. A., and Lewis, M. W. (2004). Critical pedagogy in the new paradigm. In C. Grey and E. Antonacopoulou (Eds), *Essential Readings in Management Learning.* Thousand Oaks, CA: Sage.

Dewey, J. (1938/1997). *Experience and Education.* New York, NY: Macmillan.

Discovery Channel. (2008). *When We Left Earth: The NASA Missions. Part 3: Landing the Eagle* [documentary miniseries, available on DVD]. Silver Spring, MD: Bill Howard.

Dixson, N. M., Allen, N., Burgess, T., Kilner, P., and Schweiter, S. (2005). *Company Command: Unleashing the Power of the Army Profession*. West Point, NY: Center for the Advancement of Leader Development & Organizational Learning.

Dobson, K. S. and Franche, R. L. (1989). A conceptual and empirical review of the depressive realism hypothesis. *Canadian Journal of Behavioral Science, 21*, 419–433.

Druskat, V. U. and Kayes, D. C. (2000). Learning versus performance in short-term project teams. *Small Group Research, 31*, 328–353.

Dutta, D. (2010). Retail at the speed of fashion. Retrieved from: http://www.3isite.com/articles/ImagesFashion_Zara_Part_II.pdf

Dvorak, P. (2009). Engineering firm charts ties: Social-mapping method helps MWH uncover gaps. *Wall Street Journal Online*. Accessed February 14, 2011.

Economist, the (2010, February 27). Data, data everywhere. A special report on managing information. *The Economist*, pp. 3–20.

Edmondson, A. C. (1999). Psychological safety and learning behavior in work teams. *Administrative Science Quarterly, 44*, 350–83.

Edmondson, A. C., Bohmer, R., and Pisano, G. P. (2001). Disrupted routines: Team learning and new technology adaptation. *Administrative Science Quarterly, 46*, 685–716.

Erickson, E. (1959). *Identity and the Life Cycle*. New York, NY: International University Press.

Ericsson, K. A. and Lehmann, A. C. (1996). Expert and exceptional performance: Evidence of maximal adaptation to task constraints. *Annual Review of Psychology, 47*, 273–305.

Fletcher, J. D. (2004). *Cognitive Readiness: Preparing for the Unexpected*. IDA Document D-3061. Alexandria, VA: Institute for Defense Analysis.

Fox, A. (1974). *Beyond Contract: Work, Power, and Trust Relations*. London, UK: Faber.

Fredberg, T., Beer, M., Eisenstat, R., Foote, N., and Norrgren, F. (2008). *Embracing Commitment and Performance: CEOs and Practices to Manage Paradox* (Working Paper 08-052, Harvard Business School). Retrieved from http://www.hbs.edu/research/pdf/08-052.pdf

Fry, R., Barrett, F., Seiling, J., and Whitney, D. (2001). *Appreciative Inquiry and Organizational Transformation: Reports from the Field*. Westport, CT: Quorum Publishers.

Gabarro, J. J. (1978). The development of trust, influence and expectations. In A. G. Athos and J. J. Gabarro (Eds), *Interpersonal Behavior: Communication and Understanding in Relationships* (pp. 290–303). Englewood Cliffs, NJ: Prentice-Hall.

Gale (2001). Erik Erikson (1902–79). *Gale Encyclopedia of Psychology*, 2nd edn. Gale Group.

Gardner, H. (1983). *Frames of Mind: The Theory of Multiple Intelligences.* New York, NY: Basic Books.

Gibb, J. R. (1964). T-group theory and laboratory method: Innovation in re-education. In L. P. Bradford, J. R. Gibb, and K. D. Benne (Eds), *Climate for Trust Formation* (pp. 279–309). New York, NY: Wiley.

Gibb, J. R. (1978). *Trust: A New View of Personal and Organizational Development.* Los Angeles, CA: Guild of Tutors Press.

Gibbs, N., Epperson, S. E., Mondi, L., Graff, J. L., and Towle, L. H. (1995, October 2). The EQ factor. *Time.* Retrieved from http://www.time.com/time/magazine/article/ 0,9171,983503,00.html

Gilligan, C. (1982). *In a Different Voice.* Cambridge, MA: Harvard University Press.

Gladwell, M. (2008). *Outliers.* New York, NY: Little Brown.

Goldstein, J. (2009, October 27). Health care (a special report)—as easy as 1-2-3? Checklists can reduce infections dramatically; the trick is getting doctors and nurses to use them. *Wall Street Journal Online.* Retrieved from http://online.wsj.com/article/SB10001424052970204488304574429 422345973600.html. Accessed February 14, 2011.

Goleman, D., Boyatzis, R., and McKee, A. (2002). *Primal Leadership: Realizing the Power of Emotional Intelligence.* Boston, MA: Harvard Business School Press.

Greenfield, H. (2010). The decline of the best: An insider's lessons from Lehman Brothers. *Leader to Leader, 55,* 30–36.

Griffiths, M. and Tann, S. (1991). Ripples in the reflection. In P. Lomax (Ed.), *BERA Dialogues, 5,* 82–101.

Hanna, S. T., Uhl-Bien, M., Avolio, B., and Cavarretta, F. L. (2009). A framework for examining leadership in extreme contexts. *Leadership Quarterly, 20,* 897–919.

Harris, A. M. (2010). JP Morgan asks bankruptcy judge to toss Lehman Brothers suit over collapse. Bloomberg News. August 31, 2010. 2:53EST. Retrieved from http://www.bloomberg.com/news/2010-08-31/jpmorgan-asks-bankruptcy-judge-to-toss-lehman-brothers-suit-over-collapse.html

Harvard Business Review (2006, February). Breakthrough ideas for 2006 [special issue]. Retrieved from http://www.prevent.org/newsletters/2006/mar/docs/HBR.pdf

Headquarters United States Air Force. (2005). *Operation Anaconda: An Air Power Perspective.* Washington, DC: Author. Retrieved from http://www.af.mil/shared/media/document/ AFD-060726-037.pdf. Accessed February 14, 2011.

Heifetz, R. (1994). *Leadership without Easy Answers.* Boston, MA: Harvard Business School Press.

Hoare, C. (2006). *Handbook of Adult Development and Learning.* Oxford, UK: Oxford University Press.

Hojat, M., Mangione, S., Nasca, T., Gonnella, J., and Magee, M. (2005). Empathy scores in medical school and ratings of empathic behavior in residency training 3 years later. *Journal of Social Psychology, 145,* 663–672.

Hojat, M., Mangione, S., Nasca, T. J., Rattner, S., Erdmann, J. B., Gonnella, J. S., and Magee, M. (2004). An empirical study of decline in empathy in medical school. *Medical Education, 38,* 934–941.

Holian, R. (2006). Management decision making, ethical issues and emotional intelligence. *Management Decision, 44,* 1122–1138.

Hunt, D. (1987). *Beginning with Ourselves: In Practice, Theory and Human Affairs.* Cambridge, MA: Brookline Books.

Jacques, E. (1989). *Requisite Organization.* Arlington, VA: Carson Hall.

Janis, I. L. (1972). *Victims of Groupthink.* Boston, MA: Houghton Mifflin.

Joseph, J., Berry, K., and Deshpande, S. P. (2009). Impact of emotional intelligence and other factors on perception of ethical behavior of peers. *Journal of Business Ethics, 89,* 4, 539–546.

Kayes, A. B. (2004). Organizational trust and upward influence in correctional institutions. Unpublished doctoral dissertation, The George Washington University, Washington, DC.

Kayes, A. B. (2007). Power and experience: Emancipation through Guided Leadership Narratives. In (Eds) M. Reynolds and R. Vince. *The Handbook of Experiential Learning and Management Education.* Oxford: Oxford University Press.

Kayes, A. B. and Kayes, D. C. (2007). Learning. In J. Bailey and S. Clegg (Eds), *International Encyclopedia of Organization Studies.* Thousand Oaks, CA: Sage.

Kayes, A. B., Kayes, D. C., Kolb, A., and Kolb, D. (2004). *The Kolb Team Learning Experience: Improving Team Effectiveness through Structured Learning Experiences.* Boston, MA: The Hay Group.

Kayes, A. B., Kayes, D. C., and Kolb, D. A. (2005). Experiential learning in teams. *Simulation & Gaming, 36,* 330–354.

Kayes, D. C. (2002). Experiential learning and its critics: Preserving the role of experience in management learning and education. *Academy of Management Learning and Education, 1,* 137–149.

Kayes, D. C. (2004). The1996 Mount Everest climbing disaster: The breakdown of learning in teams, *Human Relations, 57,* 1263–1284

Kayes, D. C. (2006a). From climbing stairs to riding waves: Group critical thinking and its development. *Small Group Research, 37,* 612–630.

Kayes, D. C. (2006b). *Destructive Goal Pursuit: The Mount Everest Disaster.* Basingstoke: Palgrave Macmillan.

Kegan, R. (1998). *In Over Our Heads. The Mental Demands of Modern Life.* Cambridge, MA: Harvard University Press.

Kegan, R. and Lahey, L. L. (2002). *How the Way We Talk Can Change the Way We Work.* San Francisco, CA: Jossey-Bass.

Keller, J. M. (1992). Motivational systems. In H. D. Stolovitch and E. J. Keeps (Eds), *Handbook of Human Performance Technology: A Comprehensive Guide for Analyzing and Solving Performance Problems in Organizations.* San Francisco, CA: Jossey-Bass.

Kerr, S. (1995). On the folly of rewarding A, while hoping for B. *Academy of Management Executive, 9,* 7–14.

Kets de Vries, M. F. and Miller, D. (1984). *The Neurotic Organization. Diagnosing and Changing Counterproductive Styles of Management.* San Francisco, CA: Jossey-Bass.

King, P. M. and Kitchener, K. S. (1994). *Developing Reflective Judgment: Understanding and Promoting Intellectual Growth and Critical Thinking in Adolescents and Adults.* San Francisco: Jossey-Bass.

Klein, G. (1999). *Sources of Power: How People Make Decisions.* Cambridge, MA: MIT Press.

Knott, M. (2009). Individual team member self-perception of team learning beliefs and behaviors: Developing a measure and testing a model. Unpublished doctoral dissertation, The George Washington University, Washington, DC.

Kohlberg, L. (1969). Stages and sequences: The cognitive-developmental approach to socialization. In D. A. Goslin (Ed.), *Handbook of Socialization Theory and Research.* Chicago, IL: Rand McNally.

Kolb, D. A. (1984). *Experiential Learning: Experience as the Source of Learning and Development.* Englewood Cliffs, NJ: Prentice Hall.

Kranz, G. (2000). *Failure is Not an Option: Mission Control from Mercury to Apollo 13 and Beyond.* New York, NY: Simon & Schuster.

Landro, L. (2010, February 16). Building team spirit: Nurses hesitate to challenge doctors even when doctors are ordering the wrong drug or operating on the wrong limb. *Wall Street Journal Online* http://online.wsj.com/article/SB10001424052748704431404575067921122148064.html

Latham, G. P. and Locke, E. A. (2006). Enhancing the benefits and overcoming the pitfalls of goal setting. *Organizational Dynamics, 35,* 332–340.

LePine, J. A., LePine, M. A., and Jackson, C. L. (2004). Challenge and hindrance stress: Relationships with exhaustion, motivation to learn, and learning performance. *Journal of Applied Psychology, 89,* 883–891.

Levinson, D. J., Darrow, C. N., Klein, E. B., Levinson, M. H., McKee, B. (1978). *The Seasons of a Man's Life.* New York, NY: Ballantine.

Levinson, D. J. and Levinson, J. D. (1996). *The Seasons of a Woman's Life.* New York, NY: Ballantine.

Levinson, H. (1976). *Psychological Man.* Cambridge, MA: The Levinson Institute.

Lewin, K. (1948). *Resolving Social Conflicts: Selected Papers on Group Dynamics.* New York, NY: Harper.

Lipshitz, R., Friedman, V. J., and Popper, M. (2006). *Demystifying Organizational Learning.* Thousand Oaks, CA: Sage.

Loevinger, J. (1976). *Ego Development: Conceptions and Theories.* San Francisco, CA: Jossey-Bass.

MacPherson, M. (2005). *Roberts Ridge: A Story of Courage and Sacrifice on Takur Ghar Mountain, Afghanistan.* New York, NY: Bantam Dell.

Maguire, E. A., Gadian, D. G., Johnsrude, I. S., Good, C. D., Ashburner, J., Frackowiak, R. S. J., and Frith, C. D. (2000). Navigation-related structural change in the hippocampi of taxi drivers. *Proceedings of the National Academy of Sciences of the United States of America, 97,* 4398–4403.

March, J. G. and Simon, H. A. (1958). *Organizations.* New York, NY: John Wiley & Sons.

Marquardt, M. (1999). *Action Learning in Action.* Palo Alto, CA: Davies Black.

Martin, A. (2010). *Everyday Leadership* [white paper]. Greensboro, NC: Center for Creative Leadership. Retrieved from http://www.ccl.org/leadership/pdf/research/EverydayLeadership.pdf

Mayer, J. D. and Salovey, P. (1997). What is emotional intelligence: Implications for educators. In P. Salovey and D. Sluyter (Eds), *Emotional Development and Emotional Intelligence* (pp. 3–31). New York, NY: Basic Books.

McCracken, M. (2005). Towards a typology of managerial barriers to learning. *Journal of Management Development, 24,* 559–575.

McGinn, D. (2007). The emotional workplace; first dismissed as a fad, employers like Air Canada and American Express now testing for EQ. *Financial Post,* p. FW3.

McGregor, D. M. (1987). *The Human Side of Enterprise.* New York, NY: Random House.

Mills, T. M. (1967). *The Sociology of Small Groups.* Englewood Cliffs, NJ: Prentice-Hall.

Morris, M. W. and Moore, P. C. (2000). The lessons we (don't) learn: Counterfactual thinking and organizational accountability after a close call. *Administrative Science Quarterly, 45,* 737–765.

National Association of Colleges and Employers. (2010). *Job Outlook 2010.* Bethlehem, PA: Author. Retrieved from http://www.shrm.org

Navy Aviation Schools Command. (2010a). CRM history and command structure (Lesson 1.2). In *CRM Facilitation Course.* Pensacola, FL: Author.

Navy Aviation Schools Command. (2010b). Assertiveness. Retrieved from https://www.netc.navy.mil/nascweb/crm/standmat/seven_skills/AS.htm

Naylor, S. (2005). *Not a Good Day to Die.* New York, NY: Berkley Books.

Novations Group. (2004). *The Four Stages of Contribution.* Boston, MA: Novations Group, Inc.

Ordóñez, L. D., Schweitzer, M. E., Galinsky, A. D., and Bazerman, M. H. (2009). Goals gone wild: The systematic side effects of overprescribing goal setting. *Academy of Management Perspectives, 23,* 6–16.

Patel, V. L., Groen, G. J., and Frederiksen, C. H. (1986). Differences between students and physicians in memory for clinical cases. *Medical Education, 20*, 3–9.

Pavlov, I. P. (1927). *Conditioned Reflexes: An Investigation of the Physiological Activity of the Cerebral Cortex*. London, UK: Oxford University Press.

Peterson, S. J., Waldman, D. A., Balthazard, P. A., and Thatcher, R. W. (2008). Are the brains of optimistic, hopeful, confident and resilient leaders different? *Organizational Dynamics, 37*, 342–353.

Phillips, S. (2006, June 26). Rescue on Roberts Ridge. *Dateline NBC*. Retrieved from http://www.msnbc.msn.com/id/13233811.

Piaget, J. (2001). *Studies in Reflecting Abstraction*. London: Psychology Press.

Pronovost, P., Needham, D., Berenholtz, S., Sinopoli, D., Chu, H., Cosgrove, S., Sexton, B., Hyzy, R., Welsh, R., Roth, G., Bander, J., Kepros, J. J., and Goeschel, C. (2006). An intervention to decrease catheter-related bloodstream infections in the ICU. *New England Journal of Medicine, 355*, 2725–2732.

Pronovost, P. and Vohr, E. (2010). *Safe Patients, Smart Hospitals: How One Doctor's Checklist Can Help Us Change Health Care from the Inside Out*. New York, NY: Hudson Street Press.

Raelin, J. (1997). A model of work-based learning. *Organization Science, 6*, 563–578.

Raelin, J. (2003). *Creating Leaderful Organizations: How to Bring Out Leadership in Everyone*. San Francisco, CA: Berrett-Kohler.

Raelin, J. (2006). Does action learning promote collaborative leadership? *Academy of Management Learning & Education, 5*, 152–168.

Reason, J. (1995). Safety in the operating theatre—Part 2: Human error and organizational failure. *Current Anesthesia and Critical Care, 6*, 121–126.

Reid, J. (2008, May/June). The resilient leader: Why EQ matters. *Ivey Business Journal*. Retrieved from http://www.ibj.ca/article.asp?intArticle_ID=762

Revans, R. W. (1982). *The Origin and Growth of Action Learning*. Brickley, UK: Chartwell-Bratt.

Reynolds, M. (1999a). Critical reflection and management education: Rehabilitating less hierarchical approaches. *Journal of Management Education, 23*, 537–553.

Reynolds, M. (1999b). Grasping the nettle: Possibilities and pitfalls of a critical management pedagogy. *British Journal of Management, 10*, 171–184.

Reynolds, M. (2009). Wild frontiers—reflections on experiential learning. *Management Learning, 40*, 387–392.

Reynolds, M. and Vince, R. (2004). *Organizing Reflection*. Farnham, Surrey, UK: Ashgate.

Reynolds, M. and Vince, R. (2007). *Experiential Learning and Management Education*. Oxford, UK: Oxford University Press.

Robbins, M. (2007). Getting in touch with your emotional intelligence: What is it, and how can employers apply it to the workplace? *Employee Benefit News, 11*, 68.

Roethlisberger, F. J. (1968). *Man-in-Organization*. Cambridge, MA: Belknap Press of Harvard University Press.

Rose, C. and Turow, S. (2010, May 19). Interview [televised on PBS]. Retrieved from http://www.charlierose.com/view/interview/11020.

Rush, D. (2002). Measuring connectivity at Aventis Pharmaceuticals. *KM Review, 5*(2), 10.

Salovey, P. and Mayer, J. D. (1990). Emotional intelligence. *Imagination, Cognitions & Personality, 9*, 185–211.

Salter, C. (2007). Failure doesn't suck. *Fast Company*, May 1, 2007. Retrieved from http://www.fastcompany.com/magazine/115/open_next-design.html

Sashkin, M. and Sashkin, M. (2003). *Leadership that Matters*. San Francisco, CA: Berrett-Koehler.

Satterfield, J. M. (2000). Optimism, culture and history: The roles of explanatory style, integrative complexity, and pessimistic rumination. In J. E. Gillham (ed.), *The Science of Optimism and Hope* (pp. 41–56). Philadelphia, PA: Templeton Foundation Press.

Schein, E. H. (1978). *Career Dynamics: Matching Individual and Organizational Needs*. Reading, MA: Addison-Wesley.

Schultz, K. (2010, June 21). *Slate*. Retrieved from http://www.slate.com/blogs/blogs/thewrongstuff/default.aspx.

Schulz, L. E. and Bonawitz, E. B. (2007). Serious fun: Preschoolers play more when evidence is confounded. *Developmental Psychology, 43*, 1045–1050.

Schulz, L. E., Goodman, N. D., Tenebaum, J. B., and Jenkins, A. C. (2008). Going beyond the evidence: Abstract laws and preschoolers' response to anomalous data. *Cognition, 109*, 211–223.

Self, N. (2008). *Two Wars*. Carol Stream, IL: Tyndale.

Seligman, M. E. P. (1990). *Learned Optimism*. New York, NY: Alfred A. Knopf.

Seligman, M. E. P. (2002). *Authentic Happiness*. New York, NY: Free Press.

Seligman, M. E. P. and Csikszentmihalyi, M. (2000). Positive psychology: An introduction. *American Psychologist, 55*, 5–14.

Senge, P. (1990). The leader's new work: Building learning organizations. *Sloan Management Review, 32*, 7–23.

Shandro, A., Mulgan, G., Brophy, M., Bacon, N., and Mguni, N. (2010). *The State of Happiness Report*. London, UK: The Young Foundation. Retrieved from http://www.youngfoundation.org/publications/reports/the-state-happiness-january-2010.

Siegler, R. S. (1996). *Emerging Minds: The Process of Change in Children's Thinking*. New York, NY: Oxford University Press.

Simpson, J. (2004). *Touching the void* (Rev. edn). New York, NY: Perennial.

Skinner, B. F. (1969). *Contingencies of Reinforcement: A Theoretical Analysis*. New York, NY: Appleton-Century-Crofts.

Snyder, C. R. and Lopez, S. J. (Eds) (2002). *Handbook of Positive Psychology*. Oxford, UK: Oxford University Press.

Spencer, S., and Spencer, L. (1993). *Competence at Work: Models for Superior Performance*. Hoboken, NJ: Wiley.

Staw, B. (1981). The escalation of commitment to a course of action. *Academy of Management Review*, 6, 577–587.

Sternberg, R. J., Forsythe, G. B., Hedlund, J., Horvath, J. A., Wagner, R. K., Williams, W. M., et al. (2000). *Practical Intelligence in Everyday Life*. Cambridge: Cambridge University Press.

Stockwell, D. C., Slonim, A. D., and Pollack, M. M. (2007). Physician team management affects goal achievement in the intensive care unit. *Pediatric Critical Care Medicine*, 8, 540–545.

Strunk, D. R., Lopez, H. L., and DeRubeis, R. J. (2006). Depressive symptoms are associated with unrealistic negative predictions of future life events. *Behaviour Research and Therapy*, 44, 875–896.

Suedfeld, P., Corteen, R. S., and McCormick, C. (1986). The role of integrative complexity in military leadership: Robert E. Lee and his opponents. *Journal of Applied Social Psychology*, 16, 498–507.

Sundstrom, E., De Meuse, K. P., and Futrell, D. (1990). Work teams: Applications and effectiveness. *American Psychologist*, 45, 120–33.

Thorndike, E. L. (1920). Intelligence and its use. *Harper's Magazine*, 140, 227–35.

Treverton, G. F. (2003). *Reshaping National Intelligence for an Age of Information*. Cambridge, UK: Cambridge University Press.

Torbert, W. R. (1972). *Learning from Experience: Toward Consciousness*. New York, NY: Columbia University Press.

Trosten-Bloom, A., Cooperrider, D., and Whitney, D. (2003). *The Power of Appreciative Inquiry: A Practical Guide to Positive Change*. San Francisco, CA: Berrett-Koehler Publishers.

Tucker, A. L. and Edmondson, A. C. (2003). Why hospitals don't learn from failures: Organizational and psychological dynamics that inhibit system change. *California Management Review*, 45(2), 55–72.

Tsay, C. H. H. and Kayes, D. C. (2010). Emotionally intelligent norms and their relationship to team learning and performance. Paper presented at the annual meeting of the Academy of Management, Montreal.

Van Susteren, G. (2009, February 12). Heroic crew of US Airways Flight 1549 (interview). *Fox News.com*. Interview Archive. Retrieved from http://www.foxnews.com/story/0,2933,491404,00.html

Vince, R. (1998). Behind and beyond Kolb's learning cycle. *Journal of Management Education*, 22, 304–319.

Vygotsky, L. S. (1978). *Mind in Society: The Development of Higher Psychological Processes.* Cambridge, MA: Harvard University Press.

Wegner, D. M. (1989). *White Bears and Other Unwanted Thoughts: Suppression, Obsession, and the Psychology of Mental Control.* New York, NY: Viking/Penguin.

Wegner, T. G. and Wegner, D. M. (1995). Transactive memory. In A. S. R. Manstead and M. Hewstone (Eds), *The Blackwell encyclopedia of social psychology* (pp. 654–656). Oxford, UK: Blackwell.

Weick, K. E. (1995). *Sensemaking in Organizations.* Thousand Oaks, CA: Sage.

White, J. and Weathersby, R. (2005). Can universities become true learning organizations? *The Learning Organization, 12,* 292–298.

Williams, M. (2001). In whom we trust: Group membership as an effective context for trust development. *Academy of Management Review, 26,* 377–396.

Wu, T. (2010, April 6). The Apple Two: The iPad is Steve Jobs' final victory over the company's co-founder Steve Wozniak. *Slate.* Retrieved from http://www.slate.com/id/2249872/

Wunderley, L. J., Reddy, B. W., and Dember, W. N. (1998). Optimism and pessimism in business leaders. *Journal of Applied Social Psychology, 28,* 751–760.

Yukl, G. (2008). How leaders influence organizational effectiveness. *Leadership Quarterly, 19,* 708–722.

Zull, J. (2002). *The Art of Changing the Brain.* Sterling, VA: Stylus.

About the Authors

Anna B. Kayes (EdD The George Washington University) is Associate Professor of Business and Leadership at Stevenson University. She has published extensively on topics of learning, leadership, and trust. She is a Faculty Fellow at the Center for Excellence in Public Leadership at The George Washington University. In addition to working in academics, she has over a decade experience in human resource management and leadership development in multinational organizations. She is author of over 20 publications.

D. Christopher Kayes (PhD Case Western Reserve University) is Dean's research scholar and Associate Professor of Management at The George Washington University School of Business. He is also a Faculty Fellow at The George Washington Center for Excellence in Public Leadership. Dr. Kayes was awarded the first-ever "most significant contribution to the practice of management" award by the Organizational Behavior division of the Academy of Management. Other awards include best paper nominations and awards from the journals *Academy of Management Learning and Education* and *Human Relations* respectively, and also the New Educator award by the Organizational Behavior Teaching Society. He is author of over 30 peer-reviewed articles and chapters and the book *Destructive Goal Pursuit: The Mount Everest Disaster.*

The Drs Kayes' approach to leadership and learning has been sought after by organizations such as Fannie Mae, Office of the Navy, Oracle, Ericsson, U.S. Army, Bank of New York-Mellon, National Institutes of Health, Federal Aviation Administration, Johns Hopkins University Medical School, The Administrative Offices of the U.S. Judiciary, Zagreb School of Management and Economics, Metropolitan Washington Area Council of Governments, Senior Executive Service Development Program, U.S. Department of Defense, Romanian Leadership Council, Hay Group, and the District of Columbia. Their website is www.learningdirectedleadership.com

Index

CPSIA information can be obtained
at www.ICGtesting.com
Printed in the USA
LVHW081650030921
696883LV00002B/174

9 780230 577541